THIS CANADIAN PUZZLE BOOK BELONGS TO

____

Canadian Animals

I	F	E	L	Y	D	P	O	R	C	U	P	I	N	E	M
P	V	O	M	D	U	S	R	U	M	O	V	V	Y	K	Z
W	A	K	X	E	I	E	C	D	G	O	T	R	T	F	X
L	X	D	P	V	H	R	N	A	M	D	O	T	D	O	E
U	E	O	C	P	E	N	C	X	R	A	U	S	E	M	I
M	G	W	O	V	G	J	S	O	X	I	R	P	E	R	S
B	Q	G	A	F	G	R	G	C	Y	K	B	T	I	M	M
E	G	E	B	T	K	R	I	R	Q	O	H	O	E	G	U
R	B	Y	T	N	S	P	E	Z	O	L	T	E	U	N	S
J	Z	A	I	O	K	Y	I	Y	Z	U	Y	E	S	E	K
A	W	M	R	U	U	V	D	K	W	L	N	N	K	K	R
C	F	P	N	P	N	H	H	A	A	O	Y	D	X	C	A
K	X	B	X	L	K	W	E	A	S	E	L	H	H	E	T
C	P	E	R	M	I	N	E	T	Q	E	M	F	A	O	E
L	P	A	R	A	C	C	O	O	N	C	Y	E	W	V	G
D	D	R	P	R	O	N	G	H	O	R	N	G	K	H	K

BEAR
CARIBOU
ERMINE
GOPHER
GRIZZLY
HAWK
LYNX
MINK
MUSKRAT
PIKA
PRONGHORN
SKUNK

BEAVER
COYOTE
FOX
GREY WOLF
GROUNDHOG
LUMBERJACK
MARTEN
MOOSE
OTTER
PORCUPINE
RACCOON
WEASEL

MAZE

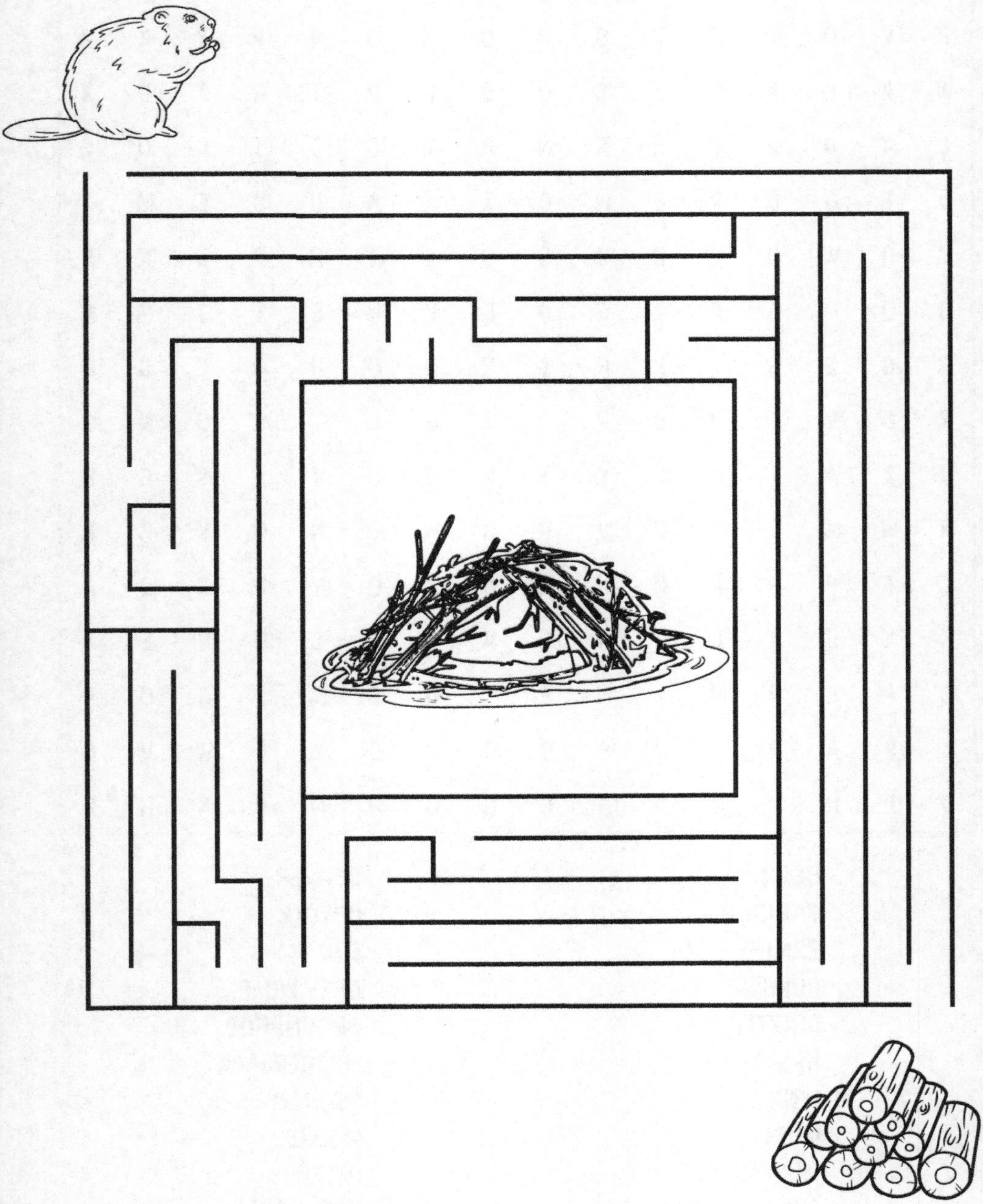

Canadian Crosswords

Solve the following puzzle based on the clues given!

Across

[3] A large, carnivorous mammal with thick fur and sharp claws, found in various parts of Canada.

[4] A large, hoofed mammal with long, slender legs and antlers, found in forested areas of North America.

[9] A large, burrowing rodent with a chunky body, short legs, and a blunt snout, native to North America.

[10] A small, rabbit-like mammal with short ears and a round body.

[12] A type of deer with large antlers, found in the northern regions of North America and Eurasia.

[13] A medium-sized carnivorous mammal native to North America, known for its distinctive yipping call.

[14] A type of bear with a distinctive, shaggy coat and a hump of muscle on its back, found in the western regions of North America.

[16] A small, nocturnal mammal with a distinctive black and white striped pattern and a gland that produces a strong-smelling spray.

Down

[1] A large, semi-aquatic rodent with a flat tail and sharp incisors.

[2] A large, carnivorous mammal with a grey coat and sharp teeth, found in various parts of the world.

[5] A small, carnivorous mammal with a long, slender body and short legs.

[6] A worker who fells trees and processes wood in a forestry setting.

[7] A large, slow-moving rodent with a heavy body, short legs, and a coat of sharp, protective quills.

[8] A bird of prey with keen eyesight and sharp talons.

[11] A small, carnivorous mammal with a pointed snout, sharp teeth, and a bushy tail.

[15] A medium-sized carnivorous feline with tufted ears, long legs, and a short tail.

Solution

Solve the following puzzle based on the clues given!

		1 B													
		E								2 W					
3 B	E	A	R						4 M	O	O	S	5 E		
		V								L			R		
		E		6 L				7 P		F			M		8 H
	9 G	R	O	U	N	D	H	O	G			10 P	I	K	A
				M				R			11 F		N		W
12 C	A	R	I	B	O	U		13 C	O	Y	O	T	E		K
				E				U			X				
				R				P							
				J		14 G	R	I	Z	Z	15 L	Y			
				A				N			Y				
				C				E			N				
			16 S	K	U	N	K				X				

Across

[3] A large, carnivorous mammal with thick fur and sharp claws, found in various parts of Canada.

[4] A large, hoofed mammal with long, slender legs and antlers, found in forested areas of North America.

[9] A large, burrowing rodent with a chunky body, short legs, and a blunt snout, native to North America.

[10] A small, rabbit-like mammal with short ears and a round body.

[12] A type of deer with large antlers, found in the northern regions of North America and Eurasia.

[13] A medium-sized carnivorous mammal native to North America, known for its distinctive yipping call.

[14] A type of bear with a distinctive, shaggy coat and a hump of muscle on its back, found in the western regions of North America.

[16] A small, nocturnal mammal with a distinctive black and white striped pattern and a gland that produces a strong-smelling spray.

Down

[1] A large, semi-aquatic rodent with a flat tail and sharp incisors.

[2] A large, carnivorous mammal with a grey coat and sharp teeth, found in various parts of the world.

[5] A small, carnivorous mammal with a long, slender body and short legs.

[6] A worker who fells trees and processes wood in a forestry setting.

[7] A large, slow-moving rodent with a heavy body, short legs, and a coat of sharp, protective quills.

[8] A bird of prey with keen eyesight and sharp talons.

[11] A small, carnivorous mammal with a pointed snout, sharp teeth, and a bushy tail.

[15] A medium-sized carnivorous feline with tufted ears, long legs, and a short tail.

Canadian History

Y	R	N	J	H	J	D	Q	N	I	A	G	A	R	A	U
N	O	R	T	H	W	E	S	T	C	E	I	V	Y	S	N
N	D	Z	T	R	N	I	V	I	G	Z	Q	S	T	O	Z
O	I	P	F	E	T	P	T	D	C	M	G	J	I	P	F
R	E	W	B	B	R	N	I	D	H	N	U	N	X	I	I
M	P	C	R	E	A	R	U	A	O	D	I	K	Y	I	R
A	P	Y	I	L	M	S	I	Y	X	M	C	L	G	V	S
N	E	Q	T	L	R	H	P	T	O	Z	A	O	L	V	T
D	M	A	I	I	T	A	K	D	O	F	X	N	O	I	N
Y	A	K	S	O	K	R	I	B	A	R	T	D	U	M	A
H	C	Z	H	N	T	P	E	D	A	S	Y	I	I	Y	T
H	O	N	G	K	O	N	G	A	I	T	B	K	S	I	I
I	S	H	S	N	D	Q	V	R	T	U	T	E	R	G	O
X	K	M	A	T	O	S	A	A	M	Y	M	L	I	T	N
H	E	F	X	R	S	P	G	H	U	L	H	W	E	G	S
B	S	G	H	N	A	M	E	R	I	C	A	K	L	W	D

AMERICA
BATTLE
DDAY
DOMINION
HONGKONG
KLONDIKE
NIAGARA
NORTHWEST
RAID
RIDGE
TREATY
ATLANTIC
BRITISH
DIEPPE
FIRSTNATIONS
KAPYONG
LOUISRIEL
NORMANDY
PARIS
REBELLION
TERRITORY
VIMY

MAZE

Canadian Crosswords

Solve the following puzzle based on the clues given!

Across

[4] derived from Inuit word nunavut, meaning our land

[5] derived from Russian word tayga, meaning forest

[7] derived from Huron word tkaronto, meaning place where trees stand in water

[9] derived from Greek word boreas, meaning north wind

[11] derived from Cree word winipeg, meaning muddy waters

[12] named after George Montagu Dunk, 2nd Earl of Halifax

[13] derived from Algonquin word kebec, meaning where river narrows

Down

[1] derived from Huron-Iroquois word kanata, meaning village or settlement

[2] derived from Iroquois word onitariio, meaning great lake

[3] derived from Gwich'in word yukon, meaning great river

[6] derived from French Mont Royal, meaning Royal Mountain

[8] named after Manitoba River

[10] derived from Algonquin word adawe, meaning to trade

Solution

Solve the following puzzle based on the clues given!

										1 C						
										A		2 O			3 Y	
										4 N	U	N	A	V	U	T
						5 T	A	I	G	A		T			K	
										D		A			O	
										A		R			N	
							6 M					I				
						7 T	O	R	O	N	T	O				
							N									
			8 M				T									
			A				R		9 B	10 O	R	E	A	L		
	11 W	I	N	N	I	P	E	G		T						
			I				A			T						
			T		12 H	A	L	I	F	A	X					
			O							W						
13 Q	U	E	B	E	C					A						
			A													

Across

[4] derived from Inuit word nunavut, meaning our land

[5] derived from Russian word tayga, meaning forest

[7] derived from Huron word tkaronto, meaning place where trees stand in water

[9] derived from Greek word boreas, meaning north wind

[11] derived from Cree word winipeg, meaning muddy waters

[12] named after George Montagu Dunk, 2nd Earl of Halifax

[13] derived from Algonquin word kebec, meaning where river narrows

Down

[1] derived from Huron-Iroquois word kanata, meaning village or settlement

[2] derived from Iroquois word onitariio, meaning great lake

[3] derived from Gwich'in word yukon, meaning great river

[6] derived from French Mont Royal, meaning Royal Mountain

[8] named after Manitoba River

[10] derived from Algonquin word adawe, meaning to trade

Canadian Etymology

P	Y	T	D	M	O	N	T	A	G	U	R	C	P	J	N
Q	T	D	A	U	G	H	T	E	R	J	O	E	Q	P	L
N	A	V	I	G	A	T	O	R	E	A	R	L	C	I	C
I	B	O	R	E	A	S	B	E	X	D	Z	Y	D	N	O
D	H	I	P	A	D	A	W	E	N	U	W	G	I	W	L
I	G	U	F	Z	B	O	C	A	I	R	S	U	W	Y	U
X	W	E	R	T	H	M	L	R	H	A	Q	I	J	Z	M
M	I	L	I	O	W	G	S	S	E	N	O	R	T	H	B
E	C	K	U	T	N	M	I	F	O	E	S	O	C	L	I
A	H	L	A	E	C	N	Q	G	T	O	G	Q	J	Y	A
D	I	V	T	E	N	C	L	I	T	L	O	U	I	S	E
O	N	F	B	I	N	A	U	K	O	Z	C	O	I	Q	P
W	O	E	F	Z	O	N	R	F	K	P	Y	I	S	L	O
A	K	Q	M	F	I	A	A	N	Y	X	F	S	R	D	W
D	M	D	N	O	U	Z	U	I	R	O	Q	U	O	I	S
S	W	F	G	X	V	D	W	G	K	A	N	A	T	A	V

ADAWE
ARKTOS
COLUMBIA
DAUGHTER
EARL
FINNISH
HURON
IROQUOIS
KEBEC
MEADOW
NAVIGATOR

ALGONQUIN
BOREAS
CREE
DUNK
ENGLAND
GWICH'IN
INUIT
KANATA
LOUISE
MONTAGU
NORTH

MAZE

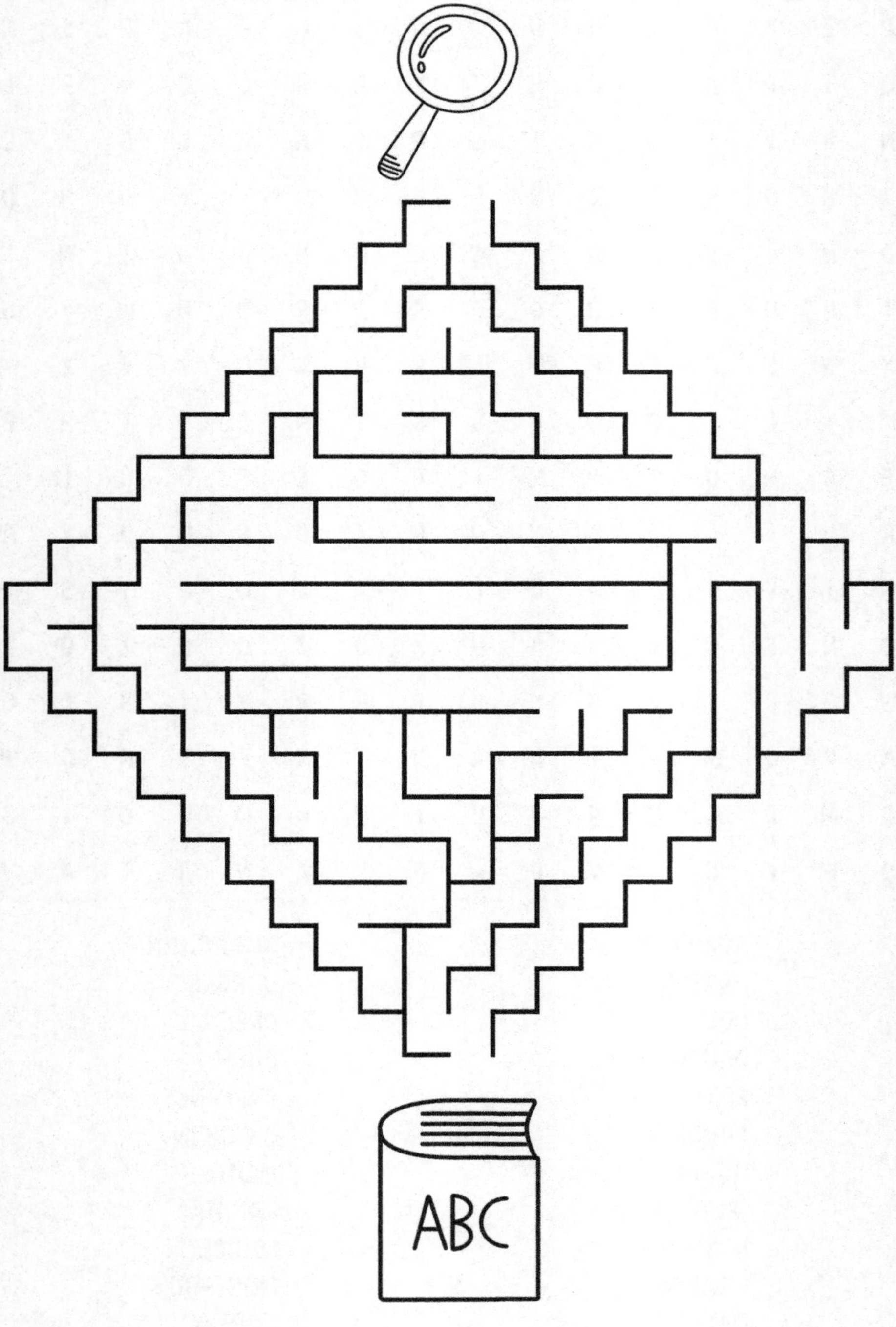

Canadian Crosswords

Solve the following puzzle based on the clues given!

Across

[2] A Native American people who lived in the eastern woodlands of North America and spoke a Huron-Wyandot language.

[4] A Native American people who live in the Arctic regions of Canada, Alaska, and Greenland and speak an Inuit language.

[5] A Native American people who lived in the eastern woodlands of North America and spoke a Cree language.

[6] The Cree word for the Saskatchewan River, which flows through the Prairie provinces of Canada.

[10] The Greek god of the north wind.

[11] A Native American people who live in northern Canada and Alaska and speak a Gwich'in language.

Down

[1] A Native American confederation of several tribes who lived in the eastern woodlands of North America and spoke an Iroquoian language.

[3] The French spelling of Quebec, a province in eastern Canada.

[7] A Native American people who lived in the eastern woodlands of North America and spoke an Algonquian language.

[8] A surname of French origin.

[9] A word in the Mohawk language meaning "village" or "community." It is sometimes used as a name for Canada.

Solution

Solve the following puzzle based on the clues given!

			1 I											
			R											
2 H	U	R	O	N										
			Q						3 K					
	4 I	N	U	I	T		5 C	R	E	E				
			O						B					
			I						E					
	6 K	I	S	I	S	K	7 A	T	C	H	E	W	A	N
							L							
		8 M					G			9 K				
		O				10 B	O	R	E	A	S			
		N					N			N				
		T					Q			A				
		A					U			T				
		11 G	W	I	C	H	I	N		A				
		U					N							

Across

[2] A Native American people who lived in the eastern woodlands of North America and spoke a Huron-Wyandot language.

[4] A Native American people who live in the Arctic regions of Canada, Alaska, and Greenland and speak an Inuit language.

[5] A Native American people who lived in the eastern woodlands of North America and spoke a Cree language.

[6] The Cree word for the Saskatchewan River, which flows through the Prairie provinces of Canada.

[10] The Greek god of the north wind.

[11] A Native American people who live in northern Canada and Alaska and speak a Gwich'in language.

Down

[1] A Native American confederation of several tribes who lived in the eastern woodlands of North America and spoke an Iroquoian language.

[3] The French spelling of Quebec, a province in eastern Canada.

[7] A Native American people who lived in the eastern woodlands of North America and spoke an Algonquian language.

[8] A surname of French origin.

[9] A word in the Mohawk language meaning "village" or "community." It is sometimes used as a name for Canada.

Canadian Geography

K	J	S	H	N	I	A	G	A	R	A	Q	Z	K	C	C
Y	N	Q	S	U	K	A	R	I	V	E	R	A	I	S	S
B	X	C	O	R	D	I	L	L	E	R	A	T	N	N	E
K	R	B	E	P	A	S	H	N	A	A	N	I	I	C	M
F	V	X	O	S	S	V	O	N	C	A	A	A	N	G	O
B	B	Y	Z	R	G	T	A	N	L	L	T	E	C	T	U
J	H	I	G	U	E	E	Y	T	P	N	R	I	S	K	N
P	Z	D	H	V	C	A	A	F	U	W	T	E	H	E	T
A	F	U	N	O	T	Y	L	O	A	C	R	T	I	W	A
C	S	A	D	O	A	U	M	L	R	O	R	R	T	E	I
I	H	K	L	S	G	Y	N	A	F	O	I	Z	O	C	N
F	I	Q	S	L	K	Q	T	D	N	A	L	A	K	E	S
I	E	S	A	C	S	D	G	Q	R	D	K	F	I	Y	G
C	L	I	O	V	D	M	T	P	I	A	U	N	A	S	F
V	D	R	Z	U	D	S	E	G	U	Z	B	B	V	D	G
T	T	A	P	P	A	L	A	C	H	I	A	N	N	U	T

APPALACHIAN
ATLANTIC
BOREAL
FALLS
GULF
LAKES
MOUNTAINS
NORTH
PACIFIC
PRAIRIE
ROCKY
TUNDRA

ARCTIC
BAY
CORDILLERA
FOREST
HUDSON
LAWRENCE
NIAGARA
OCEAN
PLAINS
RIVER
SHIELD

MAZE

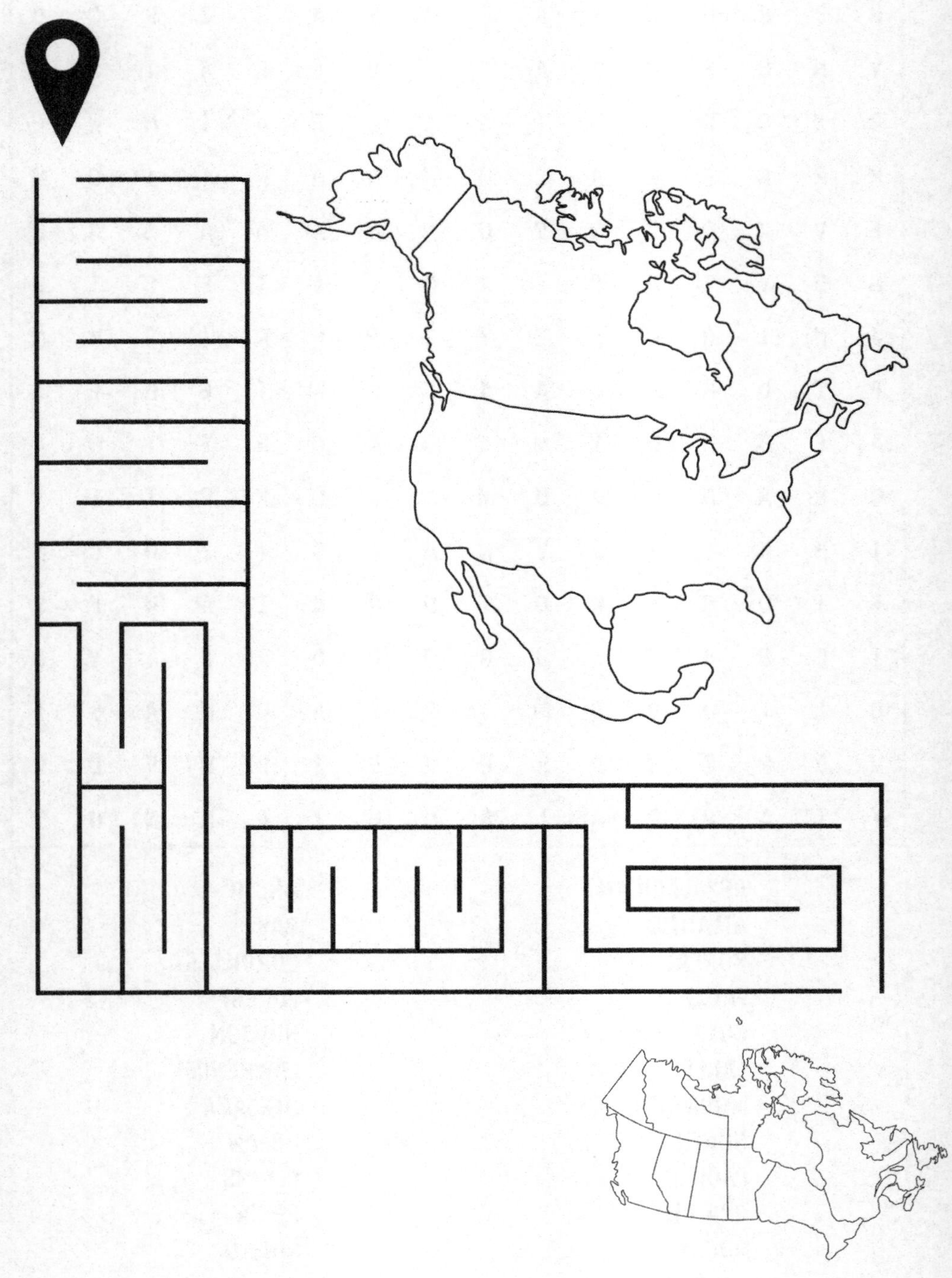

Canadian Crosswords

Solve the following puzzle based on the clues given!

Across

[3] A wide, flat region of land with few trees, often grassland or prairie.

[4] A large body of saltwater located in northeastern Canada, known for its cold, icy conditions and its rich wildlife.

[6] A type of forest found in the northern regions of North America and Eurasia, characterized by coniferous trees and a long, cold winter.

[8] A cold, treeless region located near the Arctic, characterized by permafrost and a short growing season.

[9] A vast body of saltwater that covers most of the Earth's surface.

[11] A wide, flat grassland found in the central regions of North America.

Down

[1] A large, partially enclosed body of water that is connected to an ocean or sea.

[2] A large, rocky plateau that forms the ancient core of the North American continent.

[5] A famous waterfall located on the Niagara River, which forms the border between the United States and Canada.

[7] A region located around the North Pole, characterized by cold, icy conditions and sparse vegetation.

[10] A direction, opposite to south, at the top of a map or globe.

Solution

Solve the following puzzle based on the clues given!

	1 G		2 S									
	U		H									
3 P	L	A	I	N	S							
	F		E									
			L									
	4 H	U	D	S	O	5 N						
						I						
		6 B	O	R	E	A	L		7 A			
						G			R			
	8 T	U	N	D	R	A		9 O	C	E	A	10 N
						R			T			O
				11 P	R	A	I	R	I	E		R
									C			T
												H

Across

[3] A wide, flat region of land with few trees, often grassland or prairie.

[4] A large body of saltwater located in northeastern Canada, known for its cold, icy conditions and its rich wildlife.

[6] A type of forest found in the northern regions of North America and Eurasia, characterized by coniferous trees and a long, cold winter.

[8] A cold, treeless region located near the Arctic, characterized by permafrost and a short growing season.

[9] A vast body of saltwater that covers most of the Earth's surface.

[11] A wide, flat grassland found in the central regions of North America.

Down

[1] A large, partially enclosed body of water that is connected to an ocean or sea.

[2] A large, rocky plateau that forms the ancient core of the North American continent.

[5] A famous waterfall located on the Niagara River, which forms the border between the United States and Canada.

[7] A region located around the North Pole, characterized by cold, icy conditions and sparse vegetation.

[10] A direction, opposite to south, at the top of a map or globe.

Canadian Climate

S	N	I	N	S	U	L	A	R	O	S	Y	Y	C	O	D
Z	T	S	I	F	O	B	O	R	E	A	L	J	J	C	L
C	I	O	C	T	S	R	W	A	B	O	H	Q	B	E	M
O	I	F	R	O	L	C	L	E	A	R	G	I	G	A	B
N	N	R	O	M	A	C	M	S	G	T	Y	C	Q	N	S
T	T	B	D	G	Y	S	Y	D	R	A	I	N	Y	I	U
I	E	I	M	Q	G	L	T	Y	D	L	J	M	G	C	B
N	R	Z	L	Q	G	Y	T	A	Y	D	M	S	B	H	A
E	I	B	B	Z	W	I	A	D	L	U	Y	X	Q	L	R
N	O	H	Y	D	D	N	U	G	A	D	Z	U	I	Y	C
T	R	R	I	I	Q	O	A	E	N	R	A	O	N	I	T
A	K	M	M	N	L	G	T	I	A	C	L	N	A	T	I
L	U	U	P	C	I	A	W	L	Q	M	U	O	R	V	C
H	H	S	F	I	L	N	O	H	W	S	W	C	G	V	P
U	Y	B	C	P	F	P	T	E	M	P	E	R	A	T	E
X	O	O	X	M	C	L	O	U	D	Y	X	S	N	O	W

BOREAL
CLOUDY
CONTINENTAL
HUMID
INSULAR
OCEANIC
POLAR
SNOW
SUBARCTIC
TEMPERATE

CLEAR
COASTAL
FOGGY
HUMIDITY
INTERIOR
PLATEAU
RAINY
STORMY
SUNNY
WINDY

MAZE

Canadian Crosswords

Solve the following puzzle based on the clues given!

Across

[1] Having a lot of rain.

[4] Having a moderate climate, with temperatures that are not too hot or too cold.

[5] Of or relating to the ocean.

[7] Of or relating to the North or South Pole.

[8] Of or relating to a continent.

[9] Located just south of the Arctic region, characterized by cold, snowy winters and short, cool summers.

[10] Having a high level of moisture in the air.

[12] Of or relating to an island or islands.

Down

[2] Of or relating to the inside or the inner part of something.

[3] Water that falls from the sky in the form of rain, snow, sleet, or hail.

[6] A large, flat or gently sloping area of land that is higher than the surrounding land.

[8] Of or relating to the coast or a coastline.

[11] Having a lot of sunshine.

Solution

Solve the following puzzle based on the clues given!

			1 R	A	2 I	N	Y										
					N												
					T				3 P								
				4 T	E	M	P	E	R	A	T	E					
					R				E								
5 O	C	E	A	N	I	C			C								
					O				I					6 P			
					R				P			7 P	O	L	A	R	
									I					A			
						8 C	O	N	T	I	N	E	N	T	A	L	
						O			A					E			
			9 S	U	B	A	R	C	T	I	C			A			
						S			I				10 H	U	M	I	D
			11 S			T			O								
			U			A			N								
		12 I	N	S	U	L	A	R									
			N														
			Y														

Across

[1] Having a lot of rain.

[4] Having a moderate climate, with temperatures that are not too hot or too cold.

[5] Of or relating to the ocean.

[7] Of or relating to the North or South Pole.

[8] Of or relating to a continent.

[9] Located just south of the Arctic region, characterized by cold, snowy winters and short, cool summers.

[10] Having a high level of moisture in the air.

[12] Of or relating to an island or islands.

Down

[2] Of or relating to the inside or the inner part of something.

[3] Water that falls from the sky in the form of rain, snow, sleet, or hail.

[6] A large, flat or gently sloping area of land that is higher than the surrounding land.

[8] Of or relating to the coast or a coastline.

[11] Having a lot of sunshine.

Canadian Trees

G	A	X	X	H	P	O	S	W	A	L	N	U	T	S	Y
T	F	Y	T	M	K	O	H	E	M	L	O	C	K	U	U
V	C	H	E	R	R	Y	P	N	T	W	V	T	V	G	U
F	B	X	K	R	T	N	W	L	E	W	X	C	E	C	U
D	I	A	W	D	I	H	L	T	A	A	M	G	W	D	A
T	O	J	P	F	G	C	O	O	K	R	L	M	B	R	S
H	M	D	B	F	N	Q	O	B	P	L	F	D	E	N	O
A	M	Q	E	R	I	A	L	N	A	I	H	F	E	X	F
R	E	Z	M	C	H	R	Q	C	I	S	N	J	U	R	T
D	W	G	W	B	I	R	C	H	W	F	S	E	A	H	W
W	F	G	K	T	L	D	V	C	G	S	E	W	A	Z	O
O	E	L	M	U	A	B	U	J	E	L	P	R	O	H	O
O	O	Z	K	U	K	S	E	O	P	D	H	R	O	O	D
D	G	F	C	I	M	M	P	A	U	L	A	B	U	U	D
T	W	I	L	L	O	W	M	E	S	S	V	R	Z	C	S
S	U	C	C	U	L	E	N	T	N	K	U	X	H	M	E

ALDER
BASSWOOD
CEDAR
CONIFEROUS
ELM
HARDWOOD
MAPLE
PINE
SOFTWOOD
SUCCULENT
WALNUT

ASPEN
BIRCH
CHERRY
DECIDUOUS
FIR
HEMLOCK
OAK
POPLAR
SPRUCE
TEAK
WILLOW

MAZE

Canadian Crosswords

Solve the following puzzle based on the clues given!

Across

[3] A type of deciduous tree, known for its distinctive leaves and sweet sap.

[5] A type of wood that is obtained from deciduous trees, and is generally more dense and durable than softwood. Examples of hardwood trees include oak, maple, and birch.

[7] A type of deciduous tree, known for its trembling leaves and smooth, white bark.

[8] A type of wood that is obtained from coniferous trees, and is generally less dense and less durable than hardwood. Examples of softwood trees include spruce, fir, and pine.

[9] A type of coniferous tree, known for its flat needles and elongated cones.

[11] A type of tree that sheds its leaves seasonally, typically in the fall. Examples of deciduous trees include maple, oak, birch, aspen, poplar, willow, alder, elm, and basswood.

Down

[1] A type of deciduous tree, known for its strong, durable wood and lobed leaves.

[2] A type of coniferous tree, known for its aromatic wood and thin, scale-like leaves.

[4] A type of tree that has needles or scales instead of leaves, and produces seeds in cones. Examples of coniferous trees include spruce, fir, pine, cedar, and hemlock.

[6] A type of coniferous tree, known for its triangular-shaped cones and pointed needles.

[10] A type of coniferous tree, known for its long needles and woody cones.

Solution

Solve the following puzzle based on the clues given!

		1 O			2 C								
	3 M	A	P	L	E								
		K			D								
					A			4 C					
			5 H	A	R	D	W	O	O	D			
								N					
		6 S						I					
7 A	S	P	E	N		8 S	O	F	T	W	O	O	D
		R						E					
		U				9 F	I	R					
		C		10 P				O					
	11 D	E	C	I	D	U	O	U	S				
				N				S					
				E									

Across

[3] A type of deciduous tree, known for its distinctive leaves and sweet sap.

[5] A type of wood that is obtained from deciduous trees, and is generally more dense and durable than softwood. Examples of hardwood trees include oak, maple, and birch.

[7] A type of deciduous tree, known for its trembling leaves and smooth, white bark.

[8] A type of wood that is obtained from coniferous trees, and is generally less dense and less durable than hardwood. Examples of softwood trees include spruce, fir, and pine.

[9] A type of coniferous tree, known for its flat needles and elongated cones.

[11] A type of tree that sheds its leaves seasonally, typically in the fall. Examples of deciduous trees include maple, oak, birch, aspen, poplar, willow, alder, elm, and basswood.

Down

[1] A type of deciduous tree, known for its strong, durable wood and lobed leaves.

[2] A type of coniferous tree, known for its aromatic wood and thin, scale-like leaves.

[4] A type of tree that has needles or scales instead of leaves, and produces seeds in cones. Examples of coniferous trees include spruce, fir, pine, cedar, and hemlock.

[6] A type of coniferous tree, known for its triangular-shaped cones and pointed needles.

[10] A type of coniferous tree, known for its long needles and woody cones.

Canadian Cities

E	S	U	R	R	E	Y	X	A	R	H	O	F	V	P	K
X	G	A	R	B	V	B	N	V	P	O	K	J	L	M	T
E	V	W	J	F	Z	I	A	Q	L	C	D	G	A	A	O
R	X	E	E	A	G	C	M	R	A	Z	N	L	O	R	S
I	I	R	H	E	X	N	E	W	R	O	T	M	E	P	Y
C	A	A	R	V	C	T	I	R	D	I	I	N	O	B	P
H	Q	W	X	P	A	L	O	N	U	A	E	O	A	N	P
M	X	P	H	W	L	S	O	Q	N	H	L	N	P	B	I
O	K	W	A	I	D	L	O	A	C	M	R	O	J	H	C
N	E	P	H	N	T	C	N	T	A	U	E	A	P	P	K
D	L	C	I	N	U	B	I	K	B	I	B	L	T	X	E
M	O	W	Z	S	C	K	Y	S	B	T	E	C	L	K	R
H	W	L	A	N	G	L	E	Y	F	U	T	C	B	S	I
F	N	P	D	E	L	T	A	I	G	D	R	E	O	G	N
U	A	V	J	L	M	H	A	M	I	L	T	O	N	A	G
F	K	G	W	K	I	N	G	S	T	O	N	Z	I	Z	T

AJAX
BURNABY
COQUITLAM
GUELPH
KAMLOOPS
KINGSTON
LANGLEY
NANAIMO
REGINA
SURREY
WHITBY

BARRIE
CHILLIWACK
DELTA
HAMILTON
KELOWNA
KITCHENER
LONDON
PICKERING
RICHMOND
WATERLOO
WINDSOR

MAZE

Canadian Crosswords

Solve the following puzzle based on the clues given!

Across

[4] The capital city of the province of Saskatchewan, located in western Canada.

[5] A town in the province of Ontario, located east of Toronto.

[8] A city in the province of Ontario, located in the Niagara region.

[9] A city in the province of British Columbia, located in the Greater Vancouver Area.

[10] A city in the province of Ontario, located on the western end of Lake Ontario.

[11] A city in the province of Ontario, located in the southwestern part of the province.

Down

[1] A city in the province of Ontario, located on the western shore of Lake Simcoe.

[2] A city in the province of Ontario, located on the eastern end of Lake Ontario.

[3] A city in the province of British Columbia, located in the Fraser Valley region.

[6] A city in the province of Ontario, located on the southern end of the Detroit River.

[7] A city in the province of Ontario, located in the southwestern part of the province.

[12] A city in the province of Ontario, located in the southwestern part of the province.

Solution

Solve the following puzzle based on the clues given!

1 B				2 K							3 A							
A				I							B							
4 R	E	G	I	N	A		5 W	H	I	T	B	Y						
R				G							O					6 W		
I				S				7 K			T					I		
E		8 C	A	T	H	A	R	I	N	E	S					N		
				O				T			F					D		
				N				C			O					S		
								H			9 R	I	C	H	M	O	N	D
								E			D					R		
	10 H	A	M	I	L	T	O	N										
								E										
				11 W	A	T	E	R	12 L	O	O							
									O									
									N									
									D									
									O									
									N									

Across

[4] The capital city of the province of Saskatchewan, located in western Canada.

[5] A town in the province of Ontario, located east of Toronto.

[8] A city in the province of Ontario, located in the Niagara region.

[9] A city in the province of British Columbia, located in the Greater Vancouver Area.

[10] A city in the province of Ontario, located on the western end of Lake Ontario.

[11] A city in the province of Ontario, located in the southwestern part of the province.

Down

[1] A city in the province of Ontario, located on the western shore of Lake Simcoe.

[2] A city in the province of Ontario, located on the eastern end of Lake Ontario.

[3] A city in the province of British Columbia, located in the Fraser Valley region.

[6] A city in the province of Ontario, located on the southern end of the Detroit River.

[7] A city in the province of Ontario, located in the southwestern part of the province.

[12] A city in the province of Ontario, located in the southwestern part of the province.

Canadian Symbols

I	F	G	J	W	O	L	V	E	R	I	N	E	L	S	H
G	H	H	F	R	P	O	U	T	I	N	E	G	K	N	O
A	M	L	O	N	J	R	A	I	L	S	N	C	L	R	N
M	A	A	U	C	Q	T	P	L	E	E	U	S	F	O	E
A	C	R	P	D	K	V	C	Z	V	N	D	E	I	C	A
C	I	A	F	L	C	E	X	O	A	Z	I	T	B	K	G
H	T	P	I	L	E	N	Y	C	P	N	I	N	E	I	A
E	S	T	G	Q	A	T	J	V	O	B	U	J	E	E	S
F	Z	O	B	V	W	G	Z	O	I	W	I	R	E	S	T
Y	R	R	E	S	A	N	T	H	E	M	C	I	D	S	A
X	C	S	A	B	J	B	X	Z	C	F	N	I	Z	K	M
D	M	C	V	E	R	E	N	J	A	O	A	O	H	I	P
E	P	P	E	A	H	A	G	E	O	L	T	E	E	I	E
M	T	I	R	V	P	W	L	L	P	J	Q	M	C	N	D
Q	X	K	X	E	T	A	R	T	A	N	R	M	K	G	E
D	D	D	N	R	H	O	R	T	O	N	S	R	C	D	Z

ANTHEM
CANUCKS
FLAG
HOCKEY
LEAF
MAPLE
POUTINE
RAPTORS
ROCKIES
STAMPEDE
TOONIE

BEAVER
EXHIBITION
GAMACHE
HORTONS
LOONIE
PLAID
RAIL
RCMP
SKIING
TARTAN
WOLVERINE

MAZE

Canadian Crosswords

Solve the following puzzle based on the clues given!

Across

[1] A fabric with a distinctive pattern of colored stripes or bands, traditionally associated with Scotland.

[5] A chain of coffee shops and restaurants found in Canada, known for their coffee, donuts, and other baked goods.

[8] A carnivorous mammal with a stocky body, short legs, and a thick coat of fur, native to the northern regions of North America and Eurasia.

[10] A nickname for Canadians.

[11] A nickname for the Canadian dollar, so called because the one-dollar coin features an image of a loon, a type of waterbird found in Canada.

Down

[1] A nickname for the Canadian two-dollar coin, which features an image of a polar bear.

[2] A nickname for the Rocky Mountains, a mountain range in western North America.

[3] A patriotic song that is officially recognized as the national song of a country or other entity.

[4] A large, semi-aquatic rodent native to North America, known for its ability to build dams and lodges out of branches and mud.

[6] A winter sport in which people slide down a slope on a board, similar to surfing or skateboarding.

[7] A winter sport in which people slide down a slope on skis, either for recreational or competitive purposes.

[9] The Royal Canadian Mounted Police, the national law enforcement agency of Canada.

Solution

Solve the following puzzle based on the clues given!

				1 T	A	R	T	A	N					
	2 R			O						3 A				4 B
5 H	O	R	T	O	N	6 S				N		7 S		E
	C			N		N				T		K		A
	K			I		O				H		I		V
	I			E		8 W	O	L	V	E	R	I	N	E
	E					B				M		N		R
	S					O			9 R			G		
					10 C	A	N	U	C	K	S			
						R			M					
						D			P					
						I								
			11 L	O	O	N	I	E						
						G								

Across

[1] A fabric with a distinctive pattern of colored stripes or bands, traditionally associated with Scotland.

[5] A chain of coffee shops and restaurants found in Canada, known for their coffee, donuts, and other baked goods.

[8] A carnivorous mammal with a stocky body, short legs, and a thick coat of fur, native to the northern regions of North America and Eurasia.

[10] A nickname for Canadians.

[11] A nickname for the Canadian dollar, so called because the one-dollar coin features an image of a loon, a type of waterbird found in Canada.

Down

[1] A nickname for the Canadian two-dollar coin, which features an image of a polar bear.

[2] A nickname for the Rocky Mountains, a mountain range in western North America.

[3] A patriotic song that is officially recognized as the national song of a country or other entity.

[4] A large, semi-aquatic rodent native to North America, known for its ability to build dams and lodges out of branches and mud.

[6] A winter sport in which people slide down a slope on a board, similar to surfing or skateboarding.

[7] A winter sport in which people slide down a slope on skis, either for recreational or competitive purposes.

[9] The Royal Canadian Mounted Police, the national law enforcement agency of Canada.

More Canadian Animals

A	F	E	Y	U	W	P	H	E	A	S	A	N	T	W	V
N	V	W	M	N	Q	H	Q	O	W	L	L	E	O	H	A
T	V	Z	H	I	K	G	O	O	S	E	C	R	R	U	Q
E	R	S	B	Y	F	P	Q	T	Y	O	R	S	D	M	C
L	L	F	A	L	C	O	N	K	V	A	D	V	J	M	X
O	G	H	X	D	U	R	W	A	P	N	K	M	L	I	D
P	Z	U	P	T	I	E	A	S	N	H	E	R	O	N	I
E	C	H	S	M	S	F	J	O	B	G	S	C	A	G	W
Z	N	O	E	A	G	L	E	A	M	O	T	P	N	B	O
C	N	T	O	X	A	G	B	J	Y	L	R	E	T	I	O
C	C	L	S	T	I	L	B	Q	A	D	E	L	U	R	D
I	Z	R	B	W	D	L	V	V	K	F	L	I	R	D	C
G	P	M	O	X	U	S	O	A	S	I	R	C	K	M	O
J	H	X	A	W	C	J	M	I	W	N	I	A	E	Y	C
R	O	B	I	N	K	U	R	A	A	C	N	N	Y	R	K
M	G	R	O	U	S	E	H	K	N	H	F	L	Q	K	Y

ANTELOPE
BLUEJAY
CROW
EAGLE
GOLDFINCH
GROUSE
HUMMINGBIRD
OWL
PHEASANT
SPARROW
TURKEY
WOODCOCK

AVOCET
COOT
DUCK
FALCON
GOOSE
HERON
KESTREL
PELICAN
ROBIN
SWAN
WIGEON

MAZE

Canadian Crosswords

Solve the following puzzle based on the clues given!

Across

[3] A small, brightly colored songbird with a distinctive yellow breast, found in many parts of the world.

[4] A small, plump songbird with a distinctive red breast, found in many parts of the world.

[8] A large, colorful bird with a long tail and a distinctive cry, native to Asia and Europe and often hunted for sport.

[9] A hoofed mammal with a slender body, long legs, and curved horns, found in Africa and parts of Asia.

[10] A small, slender bird of prey with a distinctive reddish-brown plumage and a sharp, hooked beak, found in many parts of the world.

[13] A small, plump gamebird with a round body and a short, pointed tail, found in many parts of the world.

[14] A large, long-necked waterbird with a distinctive honking call, known for its webbed feet and its habit of migrating in large flocks.

[15] A nocturnal bird of prey with large, forward-facing eyes, a sharp beak, and a silent flight, found in many parts of the world.

Down

[1] A waterbird with a round body, short legs, and webbed feet, known for its ability to swim and dive.

[2] A bird with a distinctive chiseling beak, adapted for drilling into wood in search of insects.

[5] A medium-sized songbird with a distinctive blue and white plumage, native to North America.

[6] A small, plump songbird with a distinctive striped head and a chirping call, found in many parts of the world.

[7] A large, powerful bird of prey with keen eyesight, strong talons, and a hooked beak, found in many parts of the world.

[11] A large, domesticated bird with a distinctive fleshy wattle and a bare head, native to North America and often eaten as food on holidays.

[12] A large, wading bird with a long neck, a sharp beak, and a distinctive hunched posture, found in many parts of the world.

Solution

Solve the following puzzle based on the clues given!

													[1]D			
							[2]W						U			
						[3]G	O	L	D	F	I	N	C	H		
	[4]R	O	[5]B	I	N		O						K			
[6]S			L				D					[7]E				
P			U				[8]P	H	E	A	S	A	N	T		
[9]A	N	T	E	L	O	P	E					G				
R			J				C					L				
R			A				[10]K	E	S	[11]T	R	E	L			
O			Y				E			U				[12]H		
W							R		[13]G	R	O	U	S	E		
										K				R		
						[14]G	O	O	S	E				[15]O	W	L
										Y				N		

Across

[3] A small, brightly colored songbird with a distinctive yellow breast, found in many parts of the world.

[4] A small, plump songbird with a distinctive red breast, found in many parts of the world.

[8] A large, colorful bird with a long tail and a distinctive cry, native to Asia and Europe and often hunted for sport.

[9] A hoofed mammal with a slender body, long legs, and curved horns, found in Africa and parts of Asia.

[10] A small, slender bird of prey with a distinctive reddish-brown plumage and a sharp, hooked beak, found in many parts of the world.

[13] A small, plump gamebird with a round body and a short, pointed tail, found in many parts of the world.

[14] A large, long-necked waterbird with a distinctive honking call, known for its webbed feet and its habit of migrating in large flocks.

[15] A nocturnal bird of prey with large, forward-facing eyes, a sharp beak, and a silent flight, found in many parts of the world.

Down

[1] A waterbird with a round body, short legs, and webbed feet, known for its ability to swim and dive.

[2] A bird with a distinctive chiseling beak, adapted for drilling into wood in search of insects.

[5] A medium-sized songbird with a distinctive blue and white plumage, native to North America.

[6] A small, plump songbird with a distinctive striped head and a chirping call, found in many parts of the world.

[7] A large, powerful bird of prey with keen eyesight, strong talons, and a hooked beak, found in many parts of the world.

[11] A large, domesticated bird with a distinctive fleshy wattle and a bare head, native to North America and often eaten as food on holidays.

[12] A large, wading bird with a long neck, a sharp beak, and a distinctive hunched posture, found in many parts of the world.

Canadian Exports

S	M	I	N	D	U	S	T	R	I	A	L	K	Q	N	Y
K	I	M	T	W	D	U	E	E	R	P	N	J	V	N	T
X	N	O	J	L	T	B	C	A	V	A	V	F	H	N	A
I	I	K	C	W	M	O	V	Y	Q	P	P	I	E	F	E
V	N	E	S	I	E	I	Q	J	T	E	D	M	E	Y	R
S	G	N	T	D	O	L	D	Q	Q	R	P	I	R	T	O
E	M	E	D	I	C	A	L	J	A	I	N	E	P	C	S
S	E	A	F	O	O	D	M	A	U	C	N	O	L	H	P
Y	F	M	E	T	A	L	S	Q	T	I	F	M	A	E	A
V	U	I	O	E	X	E	E	S	H	N	O	I	S	M	C
E	R	B	S	I	Q	E	A	C	W	J	O	N	T	I	E
N	L	P	J	H	T	G	A	B	A	H	D	E	I	C	V
E	U	E	D	A	I	M	L	U	K	X	B	R	C	A	C
R	M	Y	E	P	D	N	W	B	N	Y	C	A	S	L	N
G	C	H	Y	C	O	L	G	V	V	K	J	L	D	S	V
Y	W	K	T	E	X	T	I	L	E	S	I	N	U	D	K

AEROSPACE
ENERGY
FISHING
GAS
MACHINERY
METALS
MINING
PAPER
SEAFOOD
TIMBER

CHEMICALS
EQUIPMENT
FOOD
INDUSTRIAL
MEDICAL
MINERAL
OIL
PLASTICS
TEXTILES
WHEAT

MAZE

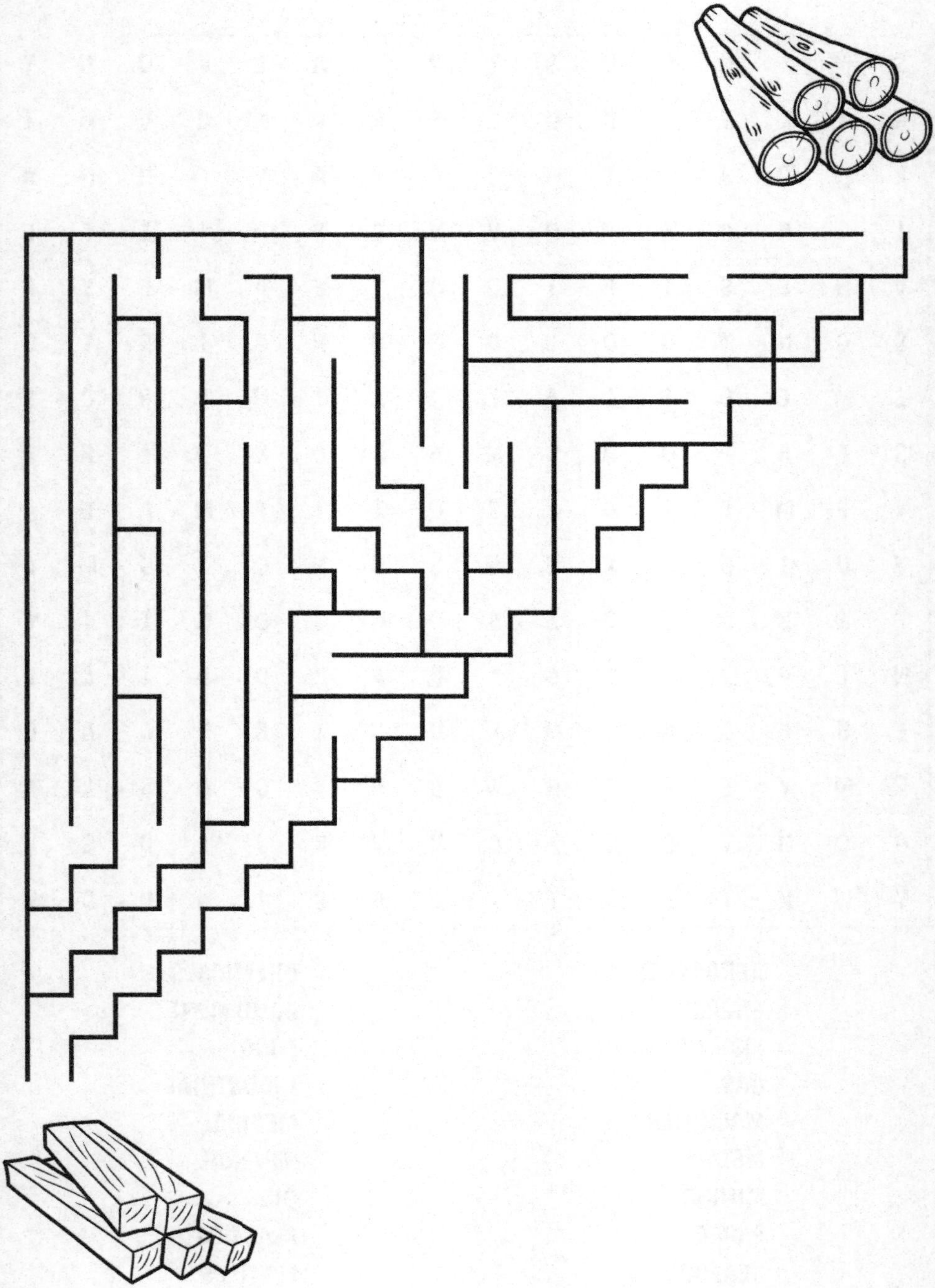

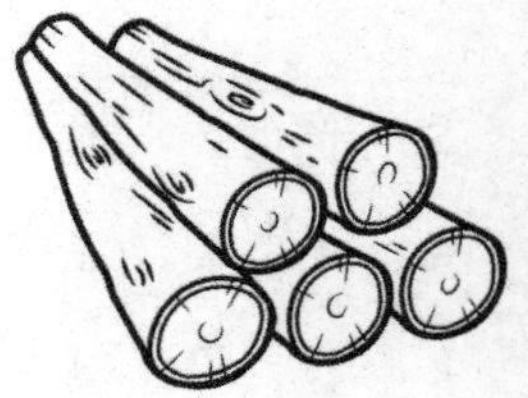

Canadian Crosswords

Solve the following puzzle based on the clues given!

Across

[4] The extraction of minerals and other materials from the earth, often using underground or open-pit techniques.

[5] The wood of trees, used as a building material, a fuel, and a raw material for a wide range of products.

[6] The activity of catching fish for food or sport, using various techniques such as angling, trapping, or netting.

[7] Elements with a high electrical and thermal conductivity, used as raw materials for a wide range of products.

[8] Motor vehicles, such as cars and trucks, used for transportation.

[9] Fish, shellfish, and other marine animals that are caught or farmed for food.

[11] A gaseous substance, such as natural gas or propane, used as a fuel or a raw material for a wide range of products.

Down

[1] A cereal grain that is widely grown for its edible seeds, used to make flour and a wide range of food products.

[2] The science and technology of designing, building, and operating aircraft and spacecraft.

[3] Of or relating to the production of crops and livestock.

[10] A fossil fuel consisting of a mixture of hydrocarbons, obtained from the ground and used as a source of energy.

Solution

Solve the following puzzle based on the clues given!

1 W															
H															
E					2 A							3 A			
A					E			4 M	I	N	I	N	G		
5 T	I	M	B	E	R							R			
					O				6 F	I	S	H	I	N	G
7 M	E	T	A	L	S							C			
					P							U			
					8 A	U	T	O	M	O	B	I	L	E	S
					C							T			
				9 S	E	A	F	10 O	O	D		U			
								I				R			
								L			11 G	A	S		
												L			

Across

[4] The extraction of minerals and other materials from the earth, often using underground or open-pit techniques.

[5] The wood of trees, used as a building material, a fuel, and a raw material for a wide range of products.

[6] The activity of catching fish for food or sport, using various techniques such as angling, trapping, or netting.

[7] Elements with a high electrical and thermal conductivity, used as raw materials for a wide range of products.

[8] Motor vehicles, such as cars and trucks, used for transportation.

[9] Fish, shellfish, and other marine animals that are caught or farmed for food.

[11] A gaseous substance, such as natural gas or propane, used as a fuel or a raw material for a wide range of products.

Down

[1] A cereal grain that is widely grown for its edible seeds, used to make flour and a wide range of food products.

[2] The science and technology of designing, building, and operating aircraft and spacecraft.

[3] Of or relating to the production of crops and livestock.

[10] A fossil fuel consisting of a mixture of hydrocarbons, obtained from the ground and used as a source of energy.

More Canadian History

J	Z	W	L	Q	F	R	E	E	D	O	M	S	D	A	T
N	H	R	N	I	E	D	G	B	L	P	J	S	Q	G	O
Y	U	T	K	O	M	A	P	O	A	E	Q	K	R	A	A
Q	F	N	D	R	N	O	M	W	T	Y	A	C	F	W	Q
Q	G	F	A	O	I	A	R	U	R	D	D	V	I	N	Y
B	S	B	T	V	C	G	T	R	A	I	L	W	A	Y	L
R	C	R	Q	F	U	A	H	L	D	P	N	N	P	T	X
P	O	W	B	Y	T	T	L	T	E	R	U	K	P	S	P
A	F	U	R	S	D	S	Q	T	S	J	I	Z	I	W	R
C	H	U	D	S	O	N	V	Q	W	C	L	S	W	E	O
I	O	C	J	U	O	V	A	C	A	D	I	A	T	Y	V
F	L	G	U	B	S	O	Q	Q	I	R	P	R	G	J	I
I	O	Y	Q	H	U	M	I	A	C	X	A	U	Q	E	N
C	A	W	I	K	E	U	R	R	G	H	M	X	R	N	C
Z	P	B	D	D	Z	V	H	L	C	K	Q	A	L	B	E
U	C	A	N	A	D	I	A	N	A	U	W	S	P	D	K

ACADIA
CANADIAN
CRISIS
FUR
NUNAVUT
PACIFIC
RAILWAY
STATUTE
TRADE

BAY
CHARTER
FREEDOMS
HUDSON
ORTONA
PROVINCE
RIGHTS
SUEZ
WAR

MAZE

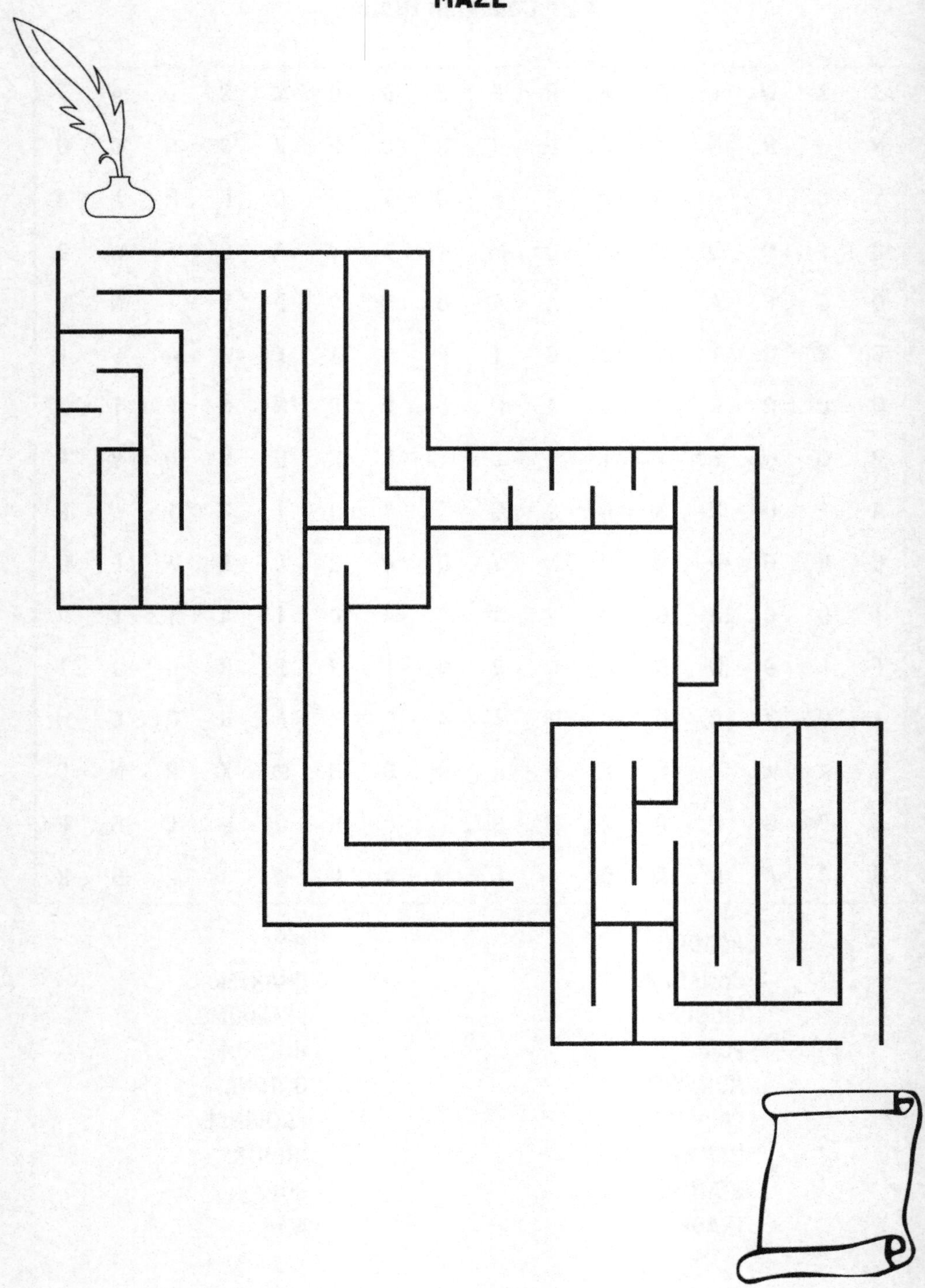

Canadian Crosswords

Solve the following puzzle based on the clues given!

Across

[5] A state of armed conflict between nations, states, or other groups.

[6] A document that outlines the principles, functions, and powers of an organization, such as a constitution or a treaty.

[7] Of or relating to Canada or its people.

[8] The state of being free from restraint, coercion, or interference, especially in the exercise of personal or civil liberties.

Down

[1] Legal or moral entitlements that are recognized and protected by law or by social convention.

[2] A region in eastern Canada that was settled by French colonists in the 17th century.

[3] A large body of water in northeastern Canada, connected to the Atlantic Ocean through the Hudson Strait.

[4] The maintenance of peace and security in a region or between nations, often through the deployment of international military forces.

[9] A town in the province of Abruzzo, Italy, known for the Battle of Ortona, a significant engagement of the Italian campaign in World War II.

[10] A political and military conflict in 1956, involving Israel, Egypt, and several other nations, centered around the Suez Canal.

Solution

Solve the following puzzle based on the clues given!

	1 R							2 A				3 H
	I							C				U
	G				4 P		5 W	A	R			D
6 C	H	A	R	T	E	R		D				S
	T				A			I				O
	S				7 C	A	N	A	D	I	A	N
					E							
					K							
			8 F	R	E	E	D	9 O	M	10 S		
					E			R		U		
					P			T		E		
					I			O		Z		
					N			N				
					G			A				

Across

[5] A state of armed conflict between nations, states, or other groups.

[6] A document that outlines the principles, functions, and powers of an organization, such as a constitution or a treaty.

[7] Of or relating to Canada or its people.

[8] The state of being free from restraint, coercion, or interference, especially in the exercise of personal or civil liberties.

Down

[1] Legal or moral entitlements that are recognized and protected by law or by social convention.

[2] A region in eastern Canada that was settled by French colonists in the 17th century.

[3] A large body of water in northeastern Canada, connected to the Atlantic Ocean through the Hudson Strait.

[4] The maintenance of peace and security in a region or between nations, often through the deployment of international military forces.

[9] A town in the province of Abruzzo, Italy, known for the Battle of Ortona, a significant engagement of the Italian campaign in World War II.

[10] A political and military conflict in 1956, involving Israel, Egypt, and several other nations, centered around the Suez Canal.

Canadian Sports Teams

O	N	K	Y	G	R	A	A	R	G	O	N	A	U	T	S
I	B	Z	S	T	R	O	I	M	P	A	C	T	A	B	D
O	L	T	W	R	N	I	C	R	C	S	H	Z	L	H	A
L	U	C	B	G	A	O	Z	K	P	X	F	R	O	A	F
W	E	U	A	U	W	P	E	Z	E	B	L	D	U	K	X
A	J	A	T	N	I	S	T	X	L	T	A	W	E	S	A
R	A	X	C	E	U	Z	E	O	P	I	M	B	T	K	H
R	Y	B	A	C	C	C	S	I	R	O	E	Z	T	Z	U
I	S	Z	N	A	S	A	K	Z	Z	S	S	S	E	M	U
O	L	E	A	F	S	W	I	S	M	F	R	U	S	B	Y
R	P	V	D	X	M	H	M	M	A	R	L	I	E	S	S
S	L	M	I	G	D	T	O	R	K	X	V	F	Z	R	J
K	F	P	E	Q	O	P	S	O	J	A	N	Z	E	F	W
K	C	O	N	D	O	R	S	C	G	H	W	L	Q	P	W
R	W	C	S	H	R	J	I	K	E	G	I	W	G	T	D
X	S	E	N	A	T	O	R	S	S	O	D	W	Y	V	M

ALOUETTES
BLUEJAYS
CANUCKS
ESKIMOS
FLAMES
IMPACT
MARLIES
RAPTORS
ROCKET
SENATORS

ARGONAUTS
CANADIENS
CONDORS
EXPOS
GRIZZLIES
LEAFS
OILERS
ROCK
RUSH
WARRIORS

MAZE

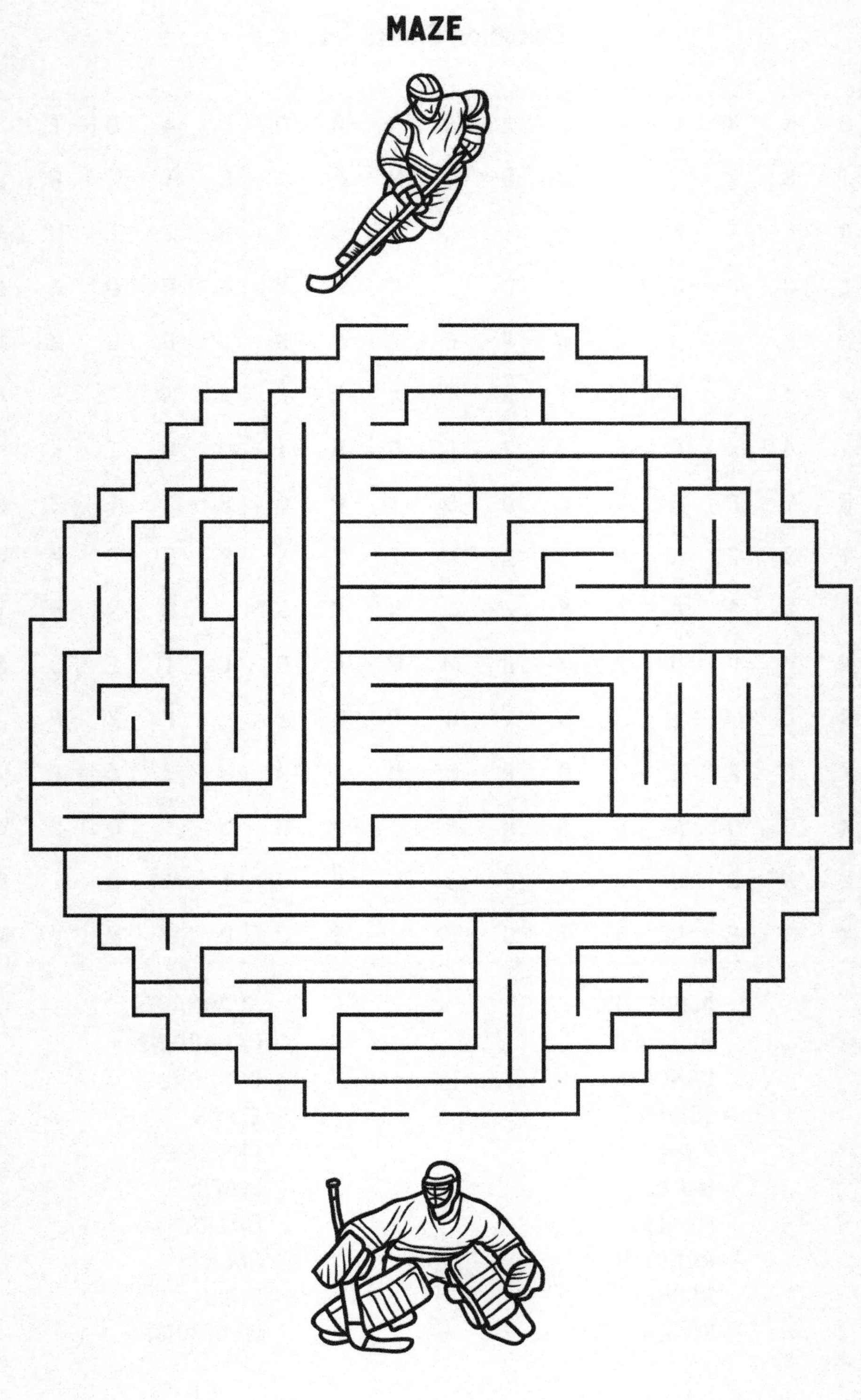

Canadian Crosswords

Solve the following puzzle based on the clues given!

Across

[1] A professional Canadian football team based in Edmonton, Alberta, that plays in the CFL.

[5] A professional Canadian football team based in Montreal, Quebec, that plays in the CFL.

[7] A professional soccer team based in Montreal, Quebec, that plays in Major League Soccer (MLS).

[8] A professional ice hockey team based in Vancouver, British Columbia, that plays in the NHL.

[11] A professional ice hockey team based in Montreal, Quebec, that plays in the NHL.

[12] A professional ice hockey team based in Edmonton, Alberta, that plays in the NHL.

Down

[2] A professional ice hockey team based in Ottawa, Ontario, that plays in the NHL.

[3] A professional soccer team based in Vancouver, British Columbia, that plays in MLS.

[4] A professional ice hockey team based in Toronto, Ontario, that plays in the National Hockey League (NHL).

[6] A professional Canadian football team based in Calgary, Alberta, that plays in the CFL.

[9] A professional ice hockey team based in Calgary, Alberta, that plays in the NHL.

[10] A professional basketball team based in Toronto, Ontario, that plays in the National Basketball Association (NBA).

Solution

Solve the following puzzle based on the clues given!

	1 E	S	K	I	M	O	2 S									
							E									
							N									
							A				3 W			4 L		
	5 A	L	O	U	E	T	T	E	6 S		H			E		
							O		T		7 I	M	P	A	C	T
							R		A		T			F		
	8 C	A	N	U	C	K	S		M		E			S		
									P		C					
						9 F			E		A					
				10 R		L			D		P					
			11 C	A	N	A	D	I	E	N	S					
				P		M			R							
				T		E			S							
				O		S										
12 O	I	L	E	R	S											
				S												

Across

[1] A professional Canadian football team based in Edmonton, Alberta, that plays in the CFL.

[5] A professional Canadian football team based in Montreal, Quebec, that plays in the CFL.

[7] A professional soccer team based in Montreal, Quebec, that plays in Major League Soccer (MLS).

[8] A professional ice hockey team based in Vancouver, British Columbia, that plays in the NHL.

[11] A professional ice hockey team based in Montreal, Quebec, that plays in the NHL.

[12] A professional ice hockey team based in Edmonton, Alberta, that plays in the NHL.

Down

[2] A professional ice hockey team based in Ottawa, Ontario, that plays in the NHL.

[3] A professional soccer team based in Vancouver, British Columbia, that plays in MLS.

[4] A professional ice hockey team based in Toronto, Ontario, that plays in the National Hockey League (NHL).

[6] A professional Canadian football team based in Calgary, Alberta, that plays in the CFL.

[9] A professional ice hockey team based in Calgary, Alberta, that plays in the NHL.

[10] A professional basketball team based in Toronto, Ontario, that plays in the National Basketball Association (NBA).

Canadian Smallest Cities

Q	B	C	C	N	L	I	O	I	P	B	O	D	M	R	G
P	S	A	A	O	A	Q	U	E	S	N	E	L	A	G	R
P	J	S	R	R	O	K	E	R	S	C	Y	R	R	L	E
O	F	T	A	H	D	A	U	P	H	I	N	A	Y	H	E
R	L	L	Q	L	I	S	J	S	M	A	L	T	S	Z	N
T	I	E	U	O	D	X	B	B	P	D	K	E	T	S	W
A	N	G	E	N	A	C	O	I	V	X	F	Z	O	M	O
G	F	A	T	S	B	B	Q	N	Q	D	C	O	W	E	O
E	L	R	T	G	G	A	N	D	E	R	Y	Q	N	R	D
W	O	F	V	C	J	B	Q	Y	Q	O	R	Z	M	R	T
S	N	A	R	O	N	G	E	X	S	O	Z	L	Q	I	S
A	J	H	L	N	E	N	M	O	T	J	X	E	X	T	T
M	X	T	P	E	D	H	G	F	C	N	Y	B	M	T	O
N	F	X	K	Y	R	O	S	S	L	A	N	D	O	G	C
E	E	X	S	D	Y	T	W	V	G	T	Y	L	H	W	V
U	X	L	R	G	R	A	N	D	F	A	L	L	S	Z	W

ALERT
CASTLEGAR
FLINFLON
GRANDFALLS
HIXON
MERRITT
OSOYOOS
PORTAGE
RONGE
SYDNEY
CARAQUET
DAUPHIN
GANDER
GREENWOOD
MARYSTOWN
NAKUSP
OXBOW
QUESNEL
ROSSLAND

MAZE

Canadian Crosswords

Solve the following puzzle based on the clues given!

Across

[5] A village in the West Kootenay region of British Columbia, Canada.

[6] A town in the Okanagan Valley region of British Columbia, Canada.

[8] A village in Oxford County, Ontario, Canada.

[9] A town in Saskatchewan, Canada, located in the west-central part of the province.

[12] A town in Newfoundland and Labrador, Canada, located in the northeastern part of the province.

Down

[1] A town in the Acadian Peninsula region of New Brunswick, Canada.

[2] A community in British Columbia, Canada, located in the Thompson-Nicola region.

[3] A town in Saskatchewan, Canada, located in the west-central part of the province.

[4] A city in the West Kootenay region of British Columbia, Canada.

[7] A city in Manitoba, Canada, located on the Manitoba-Saskatchewan border.

[10] A town in Manitoba, Canada, located in the Parkland region.

[11] A town in Saskatchewan, Canada, located in the central part of the province.

Solution

Solve the following puzzle based on the clues given!

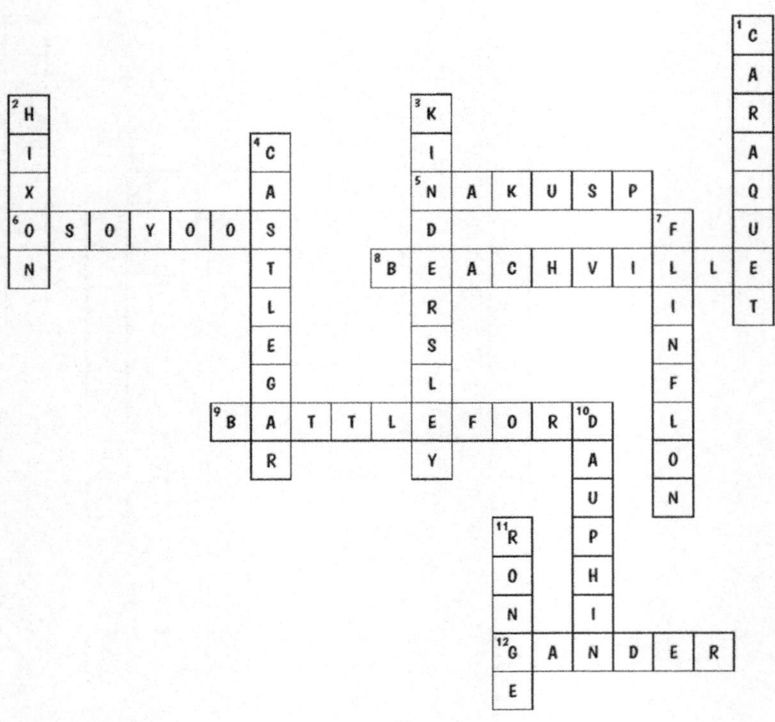

Across

[5] A village in the West Kootenay region of British Columbia, Canada.

[6] A town in the Okanagan Valley region of British Columbia, Canada.

[8] A village in Oxford County, Ontario, Canada.

[9] A town in Saskatchewan, Canada, located in the west-central part of the province.

[12] A town in Newfoundland and Labrador, Canada, located in the northeastern part of the province.

Down

[1] A town in the Acadian Peninsula region of New Brunswick, Canada.

[2] A community in British Columbia, Canada, located in the Thompson-Nicola region.

[3] A town in Saskatchewan, Canada, located in the west-central part of the province.

[4] A city in the West Kootenay region of British Columbia, Canada.

[7] A city in Manitoba, Canada, located on the Manitoba-Saskatchewan border.

[10] A town in Manitoba, Canada, located in the Parkland region.

[11] A town in Saskatchewan, Canada, located in the central part of the province.

Canadian Lakes

W	I	N	N	I	P	E	G	C	H	I	L	K	O	U	B
X	R	K	I	N	B	A	S	K	E	T	U	H	O	O	R
A	N	I	P	I	G	O	N	K	R	G	W	U	A	E	G
R	H	E	I	F	W	Y	Q	O	N	G	I	R	N	S	O
R	P	E	R	G	A	S	E	I	S	S	L	O	R	Z	O
O	V	I	J	I	S	N	H	X	D	R	L	N	W	I	C
W	B	J	V	U	E	C	I	O	L	S	I	T	R	N	G
Q	V	A	T	G	I	M	O	J	S	W	S	A	U	I	S
X	J	L	B	H	E	W	I	I	W	Y	T	S	O	M	U
O	U	S	C	I	O	R	O	L	A	N	O	E	Y	U	P
C	Y	U	M	V	N	C	I	N	O	N	N	K	B	S	E
Q	O	Z	L	M	N	E	E	E	Q	A	N	O	Z	K	R
C	G	B	O	A	A	T	H	A	B	A	S	C	A	O	I
U	K	G	R	S	O	J	N	I	P	I	G	O	N	K	O
A	Z	F	Y	O	E	S	I	M	C	O	E	R	A	A	R
U	L	E	K	Q	U	E	S	N	E	L	U	W	H	D	U

ARROW
BABINE
COUCHICHING
ERIE
HURON
KOOTENAY
NIPIGON
QUESNEL
SUPERIOR
WILLISTON
WOODS

ATHABASCA
CHILKO
CULTUS
FRANCOIS
KINBASKET
MUSKOKA
ONTARIO
SIMCOE
TASEKO
WINNIPEG

MAZE

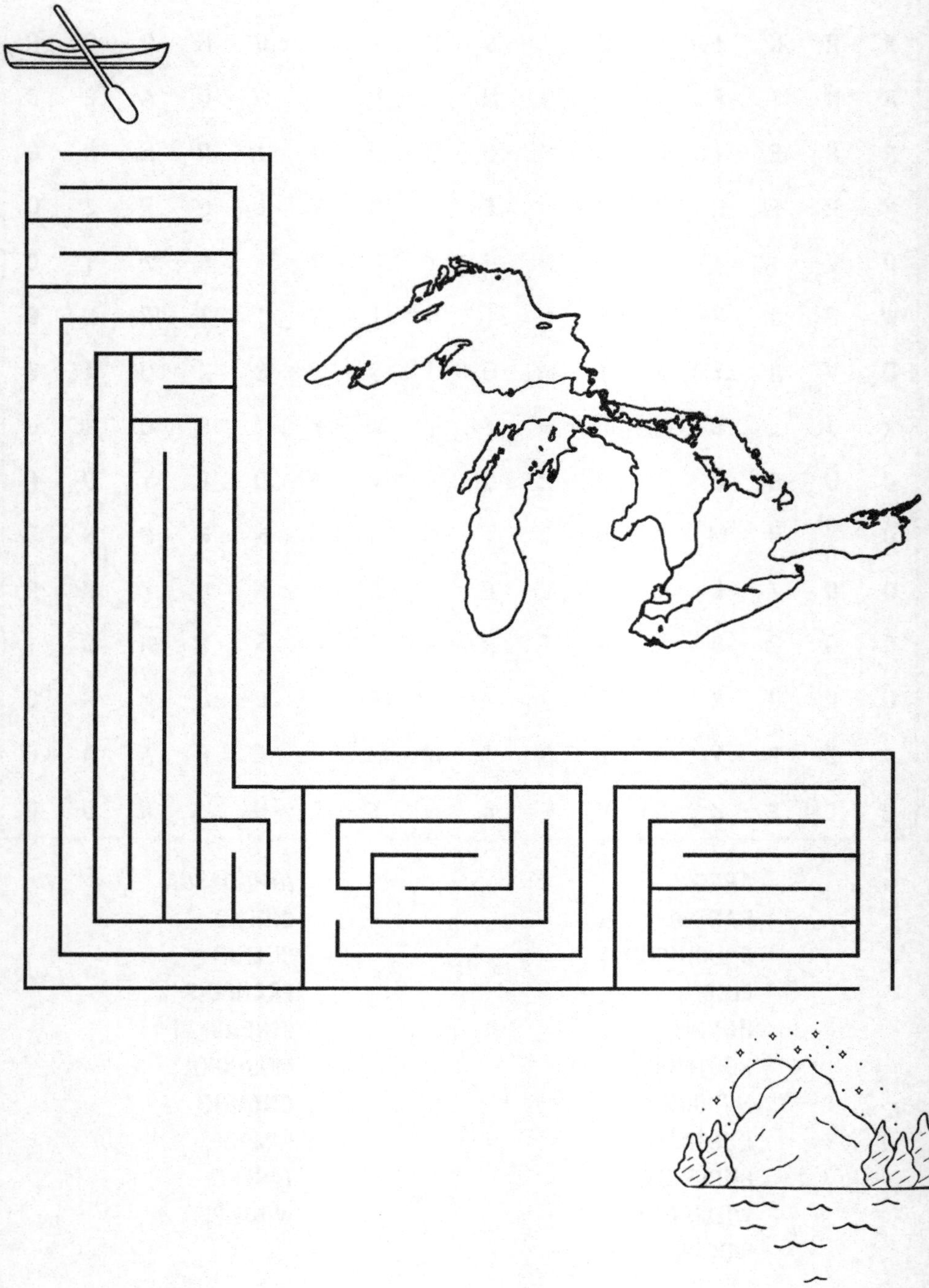

Canadian Crosswords

Solve the following puzzle based on the clues given!

Across

[1] A nickname for the Toronto Woodbine Racetrack, a thoroughbred horse racing track in Toronto, Ontario, Canada.

[3] A town in Alberta, Canada, located in the central part of the province.

[8] A town in Ontario, Canada, located in the Thunder Bay District.

[11] The largest of the Great Lakes, located on the border between the United States and Canada.

[12] A town in Ontario, Canada, located in the Thunder Bay District.

Down

[2] One of the Great Lakes, located on the border between the United States and Canada.

[4] A lake in Ontario, Canada, located in the Muskoka region.

[5] One of the Great Lakes, located on the border between the United States and Canada.

[6] The capital and largest city of Manitoba, Canada, located in the central part of the province.

[7] A town in Ontario, Canada, located in the Norfolk County.

[9] A region in Ontario, Canada, known for its lakes and resorts.

[10] One of the Great Lakes, located on the border between the United States and Canada.

Solution

Solve the following puzzle based on the clues given!

<table>
<tr><td></td><td></td><td></td><td></td><td>1 W</td><td>2 O</td><td>O</td><td>D</td><td>S</td><td></td><td></td><td></td><td></td><td></td></tr>
<tr><td></td><td></td><td></td><td></td><td></td><td>N</td><td></td><td></td><td></td><td></td><td></td><td></td><td></td><td></td></tr>
<tr><td></td><td></td><td></td><td></td><td>3 A</td><td>T</td><td>H</td><td>A</td><td>B</td><td>A</td><td>S</td><td>4 C</td><td>A</td><td></td></tr>
<tr><td></td><td></td><td></td><td></td><td></td><td>A</td><td></td><td></td><td></td><td></td><td></td><td>O</td><td></td><td></td></tr>
<tr><td></td><td>5 E</td><td></td><td></td><td></td><td>R</td><td></td><td></td><td></td><td>6 W</td><td></td><td>U</td><td></td><td></td></tr>
<tr><td></td><td>R</td><td></td><td>7 S</td><td></td><td>I</td><td></td><td></td><td></td><td>I</td><td></td><td>C</td><td></td><td></td></tr>
<tr><td>8 N</td><td>I</td><td>P</td><td>I</td><td>G</td><td>O</td><td>N</td><td></td><td></td><td>N</td><td></td><td>H</td><td></td><td></td></tr>
<tr><td></td><td>E</td><td></td><td>M</td><td></td><td></td><td></td><td></td><td></td><td>N</td><td></td><td>I</td><td></td><td></td></tr>
<tr><td></td><td></td><td></td><td>C</td><td></td><td></td><td>9 M</td><td></td><td></td><td>I</td><td></td><td>C</td><td></td><td>10 H</td></tr>
<tr><td></td><td></td><td></td><td>O</td><td></td><td></td><td>U</td><td></td><td></td><td>P</td><td></td><td>H</td><td></td><td>U</td></tr>
<tr><td></td><td></td><td></td><td>E</td><td></td><td></td><td>11 S</td><td>U</td><td>P</td><td>E</td><td>R</td><td>I</td><td>O</td><td>R</td></tr>
<tr><td></td><td></td><td></td><td></td><td></td><td></td><td>K</td><td></td><td></td><td>G</td><td></td><td>N</td><td></td><td>O</td></tr>
<tr><td></td><td>12 N</td><td>I</td><td>P</td><td>I</td><td>G</td><td>O</td><td>N</td><td></td><td></td><td></td><td>G</td><td></td><td>N</td></tr>
<tr><td></td><td></td><td></td><td></td><td></td><td></td><td>K</td><td></td><td></td><td></td><td></td><td></td><td></td><td></td></tr>
<tr><td></td><td></td><td></td><td></td><td></td><td></td><td>A</td><td></td><td></td><td></td><td></td><td></td><td></td><td></td></tr>
</table>

Across

[1] A nickname for the Toronto Woodbine Racetrack, a thoroughbred horse racing track in Toronto, Ontario, Canada.

[3] A town in Alberta, Canada, located in the central part of the province.

[8] A town in Ontario, Canada, located in the Thunder Bay District.

[11] The largest of the Great Lakes, located on the border between the United States and Canada.

[12] A town in Ontario, Canada, located in the Thunder Bay District.

Down

[2] One of the Great Lakes, located on the border between the United States and Canada.

[4] A lake in Ontario, Canada, located in the Muskoka region.

[5] One of the Great Lakes, located on the border between the United States and Canada.

[6] The capital and largest city of Manitoba, Canada, located in the central part of the province.

[7] A town in Ontario, Canada, located in the Norfolk County.

[9] A region in Ontario, Canada, known for its lakes and resorts.

[10] One of the Great Lakes, located on the border between the United States and Canada.

More Canadian Etymology

U	T	R	E	E	L	E	S	S	E	H	P	S	I	B	D
W	Y	T	K	A	R	O	N	T	O	K	L	C	I	E	E
A	T	O	B	V	Q	N	N	N	Z	Z	A	O	C	T	P
T	T	C	S	B	O	A	O	M	H	K	I	T	B	A	R
E	W	E	Q	A	I	I	P	R	S	N	N	L	V	Y	A
R	F	A	M	S	T	Z	D	R	O	E	X	A	X	G	I
H	B	N	S	A	L	T	S	D	I	C	Q	N	N	A	R
D	J	U	L	Y	B	R	N	E	M	N	K	D	Q	N	I
D	R	E	P	K	T	I	H	I	N	Y	C	Y	E	L	E
T	R	Y	V	A	W	U	T	Z	B	P	S	E	A	D	G
E	J	O	I	P	C	O	N	I	O	I	U	Y	S	Z	K
R	F	L	L	Z	F	I	R	T	U	Q	O	L	K	S	F
R	A	C	L	W	X	I	F	S	U	R	Q	W	S	C	B
A	U	R	A	B	L	Y	Q	I	R	R	E	F	O	X	K
I	B	U	G	K	U	R	S	A	C	T	I	L	R	A	Q
N	H	G	E	J	S	E	T	T	L	E	M	E	N	T	D

OCEAN
PLAIN
PRINCESS
RELATION
ROYAL
SCOTLAND
TAYGA
TKARONTO
TUNTURI
VILLAGE
WIND
PACIFIC
PRAIRIE
QUEEN
ROCKY
RUSSIAN
SETTLEMENT
TERRAIN
TREELESS
URSA
WATER

MAZE

Canadian Crosswords

Solve the following puzzle based on the clues given!

Across

[2] A group of Indigenous peoples who live in the Arctic regions of Canada, Alaska, and Greenland.

[4] A person who navigates, or directs the course of a ship or aircraft.

[5] The Algonquin name for Quebec, a province in eastern Canada.

[6] The Indigenous name for Canada, used by the Iroquois and other Native American tribes.

[7] A city in Alberta, Canada, located in the Banff National Park.

[8] A Native American tribe that lived in the Great Lakes region of North America.

[10] A low-lying area of grassland, often near a river or stream.

Down

[1] The Cree name for Saskatchewan, a province in western Canada.

[3] A town in the Eastern Cape province of South Africa.

[9] The direction opposite to the south, or the region to the north of a particular location.

Solution

Solve the following puzzle based on the clues given!

					1 K										
					I										
					S										
		2 I	N	U	I	T									
					S										
					K						3 M				
				4 N	A	V	I	G	A	T	O	R			
					T						N				
	5 K	E	B	E	C						T				
					H					6 K	A	N	A	T	A
7 L	O	U	I	S	E						G				
					W					8 H	U	R	O	9 N	
			10 M	E	A	D	O	W						O	
					N									R	
														T	
														H	

Across

[2] A group of Indigenous peoples who live in the Arctic regions of Canada, Alaska, and Greenland.

[4] A person who navigates, or directs the course of a ship or aircraft.

[5] The Algonquin name for Quebec, a province in eastern Canada.

[6] The Indigenous name for Canada, used by the Iroquois and other Native American tribes.

[7] A city in Alberta, Canada, located in the Banff National Park.

[8] A Native American tribe that lived in the Great Lakes region of North America.

[10] A low-lying area of grassland, often near a river or stream.

Down

[1] The Cree name for Saskatchewan, a province in western Canada.

[3] A town in the Eastern Cape province of South Africa.

[9] The direction opposite to the south, or the region to the north of a particular location.

More Canadian Lakes

Z	M	E	D	I	C	I	N	E	R	L	M	Z	K	C	A
B	M	A	N	D	N	P	H	C	E	N	T	R	A	L	R
C	Y	Y	J	K	A	S	Q	K	V	W	M	A	R	L	W
Y	S	H	U	S	W	A	P	H	G	L	G	S	Y	I	I
U	U	W	T	M	V	U	W	N	O	R	Q	A	D	V	L
A	H	O	I	A	O	L	B	M	U	R	E	E	N	I	L
W	O	O	U	S	F	N	D	Q	A	X	S	E	B	H	I
H	M	T	U	L	T	U	W	T	M	L	C	E	N	D	A
I	O	U	O	S	E	A	L	A	A	U	I	X	F	G	M
S	S	J	T	B	T	S	R	K	W	E	R	G	X	L	S
T	Q	M	J	A	A	O	S	I	Y	N	K	T	N	H	Y
L	U	E	U	X	W	I	N	E	A	B	W	U	L	E	D
E	I	T	L	R	K	E	F	J	R	Z	A	A	Q	E	J
R	T	P	I	M	I	Y	E	M	X	V	I	Z	K	H	P
Y	O	C	E	R	S	E	E	L	J	E	L	H	Z	I	G
K	J	A	S	P	E	R	L	D	X	L	R	W	K	L	U

CENTRAL
HORSEFLY
JASPER
KWAI
MALIGNE
MEDICINE
MURIEL
OOTSA
TAWEEL
WHISTLER
WISTARIA

GREEN
HOUSTON
KISKA
LESSER
MARL
MOSQUITO
MURTLE
SHUSWAP
TOBA
WILLIAMS

MAZE

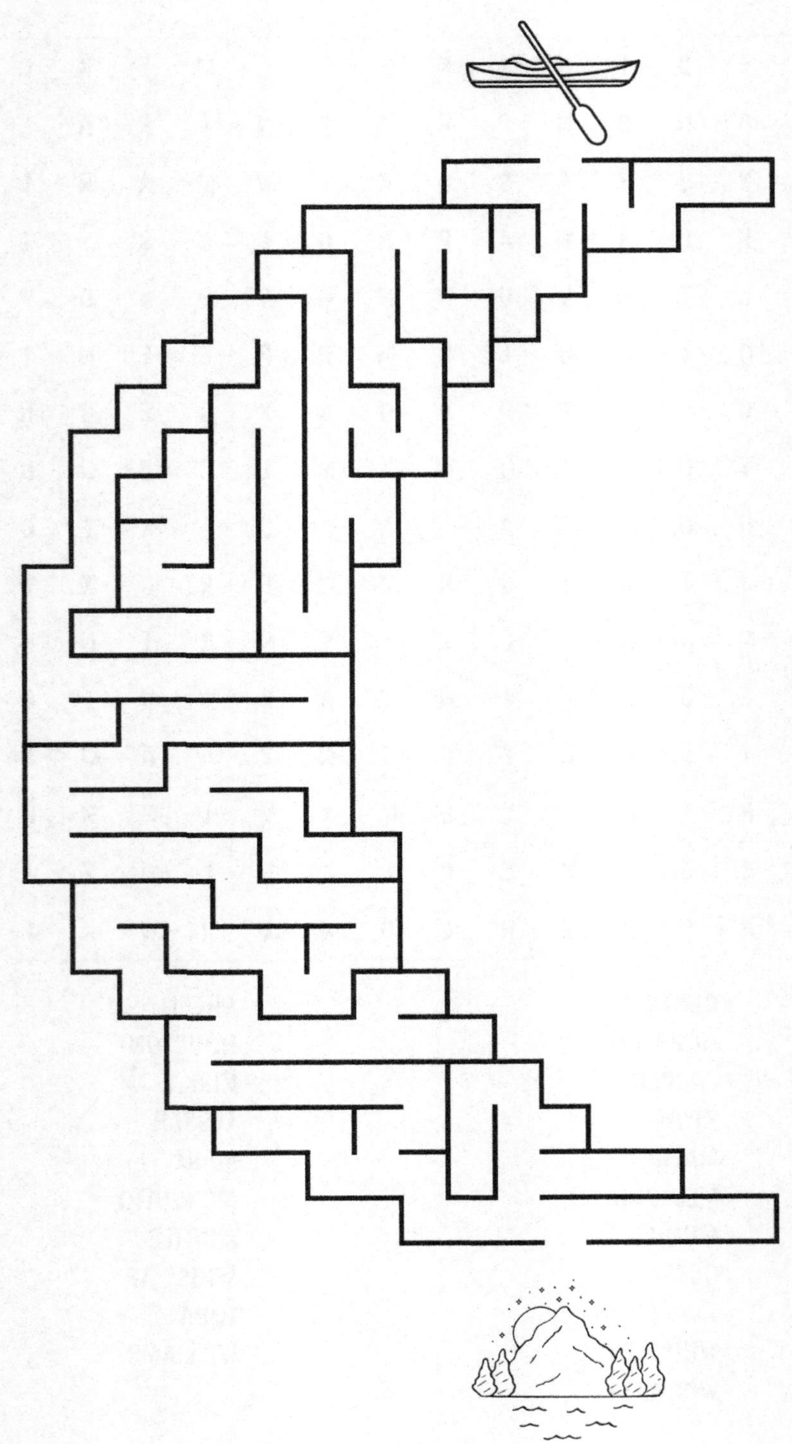

Canadian Crosswords

Solve the following puzzle based on the clues given!

Across

[1] A lake in British Columbia, Canada, located in the West Chilcotin region.

[4] A lake in British Columbia, Canada, located in the West Chilcotin region.

[6] A lake in British Columbia, Canada, located in the West Chilcotin region.

[8] A lake in British Columbia, Canada, located in the West Chilcotin region.

[9] A lake in British Columbia, Canada, located in the Thompson-Okanagan region.

[11] A resort town in British Columbia, Canada, located in the Coast Mountains.

[12] A lake in Alberta, Canada, located in the Jasper National Park.

Down

[2] A lake in British Columbia, Canada, located in the Thompson-Okanagan region.

[3] A lake in British Columbia, Canada, located in the West Chilcotin region.

[5] An island in the Aleutian Islands of Alaska, United States.

[6] A lake in British Columbia, Canada, located in the West Chilcotin region.

[7] A lake in British Columbia, Canada, located in the West Chilcotin region.

[10] A sedimentary rock made up of clay and calcium carbonate, often used as a fertilizer.

Solution

Solve the following puzzle based on the clues given!

										[1] L	E	[2] S	S	E	R

Across

[1] A lake in British Columbia, Canada, located in the West Chilcotin region.

[4] A lake in British Columbia, Canada, located in the West Chilcotin region.

[6] A lake in British Columbia, Canada, located in the West Chilcotin region.

[8] A lake in British Columbia, Canada, located in the West Chilcotin region.

[9] A lake in British Columbia, Canada, located in the Thompson-Okanagan region.

[11] A resort town in British Columbia, Canada, located in the Coast Mountains.

[12] A lake in Alberta, Canada, located in the Jasper National Park.

Down

[2] A lake in British Columbia, Canada, located in the Thompson-Okanagan region.

[3] A lake in British Columbia, Canada, located in the West Chilcotin region.

[5] An island in the Aleutian Islands of Alaska, United States.

[6] A lake in British Columbia, Canada, located in the West Chilcotin region.

[7] A lake in British Columbia, Canada, located in the West Chilcotin region.

[10] A sedimentary rock made up of clay and calcium carbonate, often used as a fertilizer.

Canadian Foods

N	P	S	J	F	N	T	I	M	B	I	T	S	S	A	K
L	Q	E	S	A	S	K	A	T	O	O	N	E	U	E	P
M	X	U	P	E	R	O	G	I	E	S	S	U	S	X	D
T	H	Z	Q	M	U	B	K	M	M	O	B	I	C	G	E
J	U	P	K	T	Y	B	S	E	O	E	A	V	S	N	O
M	U	B	A	K	S	R	A	M	T	N	K	N	D	N	T
D	X	T	E	G	A	M	T	N	N	C	A	U	E	A	M
L	P	K	G	S	U	I	O	O	N	C	H	L	L	N	N
O	Y	I	E	S	L	F	Y	N	I	O	P	U	H	A	A
B	J	A	R	P	C	A	B	M	T	A	C	L	P	I	N
S	C	T	S	O	M	H	M	R	M	R	W	K	E	M	A
T	M	D	Y	U	R	E	I	Q	E	A	E	M	F	O	I
E	N	W	V	T	P	P	X	L	K	W	D	A	C	B	M
R	B	A	F	I	I	M	T	D	L	N	I	Q	L	A	O
I	Z	C	Z	N	P	E	A	S	O	U	P	S	F	R	Z
O	B	P	B	E	A	V	E	R	T	A	I	L	S	P	B

BANNOCK
BREWIS
JIGGS
LOBSTER
MAYONNAISE
MOOSE
NANAIMOBAR
PEMMICAN
POUTINE
SPLIT

BEAVERTAILS
CAESARS
KETCHUP
MAPLE
MONTREAL
NANAIMO
PEASOUP
PEROGIES
SASKATOON
TIMBITS

MAZE

Canadian Crosswords

Solve the following puzzle based on the clues given!

Across

[4] Small, doughnut-shaped pastries sold by the Canadian fast food chain Tim Hortons.

[6] A type of pastry made by stretching dough and frying it in the shape of a beaver's tail.

[8] A type of bread roll with a split top, often used for sandwiches.

[9] A traditional Newfoundland and Labrador dish made with hardtack and either salt beef or cod.

Down

[1] A type of meat pie traditionally made with ground pork and spices.

[2] A type of food made with dried meat, fat, and dried fruit.

[3] A popular Canadian dish made with french fries, cheese curds, and gravy.

[5] A cocktail made with vodka, Clamato juice, and various spices.

[6] A type of flatbread made with flour, baking powder, and shortening.

[7] A traditional Newfoundland and Labrador dish made with boiled salted beef and vegetables, served with pease pudding.

Solution

Solve the following puzzle based on the clues given!

					[1] T									
		[2] P			O									
		E			U									
		M			R			[3] P						
[4] T	I	M	B	I	T	S		O		[5] C				
		I			I			U		A				
		C			È			T		E				
[6] B	E	A	V	E	R	T	A	I	L	S				
A		N			E			N		A				
N								E		R			[7] J	
N										[8] S	P	L	I	T
O													G	
C													G	
K								[9] B	R	E	W	I	S	

Across

[4] Small, doughnut-shaped pastries sold by the Canadian fast food chain Tim Hortons.

[6] A type of pastry made by stretching dough and frying it in the shape of a beaver's tail.

[8] A type of bread roll with a split top, often used for sandwiches.

[9] A traditional Newfoundland and Labrador dish made with hardtack and either salt beef or cod.

Down

[1] A type of meat pie traditionally made with ground pork and spices.

[2] A type of food made with dried meat, fat, and dried fruit.

[3] A popular Canadian dish made with french fries, cheese curds, and gravy.

[5] A cocktail made with vodka, Clamato juice, and various spices.

[6] A type of flatbread made with flour, baking powder, and shortening.

[7] A traditional Newfoundland and Labrador dish made with boiled salted beef and vegetables, served with pease pudding.

Canadian Inventions

E	L	S	N	O	W	B	L	O	W	E	R	W	T	T	N
F	T	A	I	C	W	Z	I	P	P	E	R	O	H	B	R
Y	C	M	N	V	P	I	B	G	P	I	P	G	Z	L	J
G	B	Z	S	D	R	I	N	R	A	T	I	X	Y	A	J
M	L	T	U	C	I	O	E	H	N	L	I	Y	Y	C	S
Q	C	R	L	O	O	D	C	A	E	S	A	R	S	K	N
G	I	W	I	L	N	L	T	R	E	K	A	R	H	B	O
I	P	R	N	E	E	S	E	N	D	L	E	N	M	E	W
N	A	O	L	E	N	T	O	E	O	K	Y	R	W	R	M
G	I	B	H	I	S	H	N	N	A	P	A	G	E	R	O
E	L	W	D	A	P	I	A	M	U	D	C	V	D	Y	B
R	L	X	O	E	T	C	E	S	A	Z	H	W	B	E	I
A	E	T	L	U	K	C	I	N	H	W	G	W	M	C	L
L	F	E	O	W	A	C	A	L	A	K	Q	Q	G	G	E
E	T	P	Z	P	F	C	A	N	O	P	E	N	E	R	I
J	I	W	I	Y	R	T	N	E	W	S	P	R	I	N	T

BLACKBERRY
CAESARS
CANOLA
CIPAILLE
INSTANTPOT
LIGHT
PACEMAKER
POUTINE
SNOWMOBILE
TOASTER
ZIPPER

BLENDER
CANADARM
CANOPENER
GINGERALE
INSULIN
NEWSPRINT
PAGER
SNOWBLOWER
TELEPHONE
WHEELCHAIR

MAZE

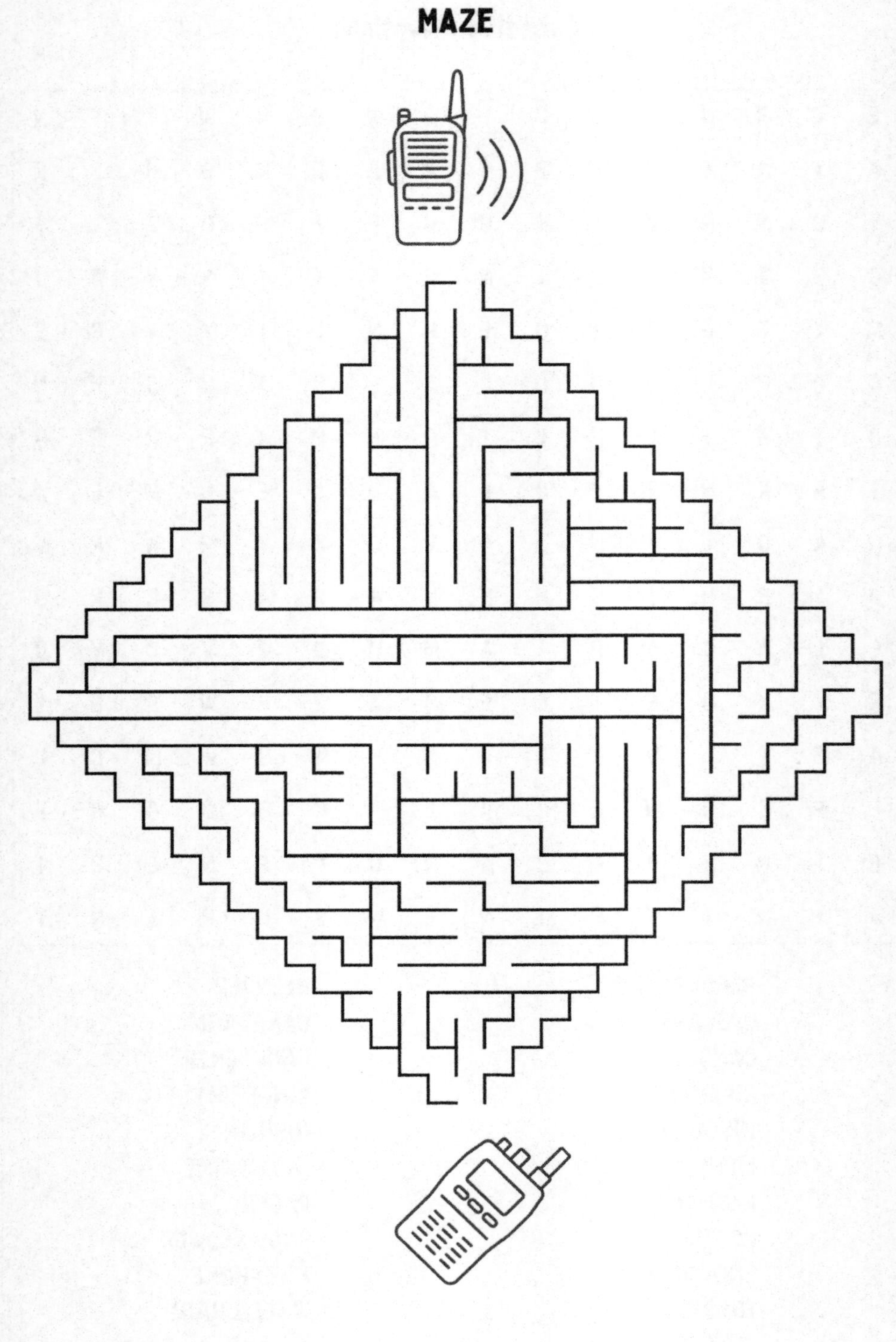

Canadian Crosswords

Solve the following puzzle based on the clues given!

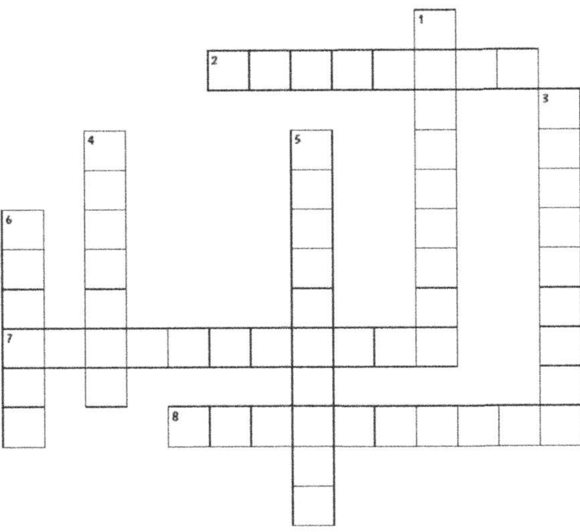

Across

[2] A robotic arm developed by the Canadian Space Agency for use in space.

[7] A tool used to apply paint to a surface.

[8] A vehicle designed for travel over snow.

Down

[1] A medical device that is implanted in the chest to regulate the heartbeat.

[3] A device used to make and receive phone calls over a distance.

[4] A hormone produced by the pancreas that helps regulate the levels of sugar in the blood.

[5] A machine used to clear snow from sidewalks, driveways, and other surfaces.

[6] A fastening device consisting of two rows of interlocking teeth on strips of tape or metal.

Solution

Solve the following puzzle based on the clues given!

										[1] P			
					[2] C	A	N	A	D	A	R	M	
										C			[3] T
		[4] I					[5] S			E			E
		N					N			M			L
[6] Z		S					O			A			E
I		U					W			K			P
P		L					B			E			H
[7] P	A	I	N	T	R	O	L	L	E	R			O
E		N					O						N
R				[8] S	N	O	W	M	O	B	I	L	E
							E						
							R						

Across

[2] A robotic arm developed by the Canadian Space Agency for use in space.

[7] A tool used to apply paint to a surface.

[8] A vehicle designed for travel over snow.

Down

[1] A medical device that is implanted in the chest to regulate the heartbeat.

[3] A device used to make and receive phone calls over a distance.

[4] A hormone produced by the pancreas that helps regulate the levels of sugar in the blood.

[5] A machine used to clear snow from sidewalks, driveways, and other surfaces.

[6] A fastening device consisting of two rows of interlocking teeth on strips of tape or metal.

Canadian Rivers

F	S	B	R	S	T	L	A	W	R	E	N	C	E	Q	E
C	E	U	C	P	R	Z	I	O	T	T	A	W	A	N	A
H	V	Y	R	T	E	H	W	A	O	X	V	S	O	D	T
U	E	I	Z	V	C	N	W	Z	R	M	L	S	I	N	H
R	R	H	S	N	O	A	S	H	S	D	L	K	P	O	A
C	N	L	E	K	W	D	N	M	E	E	I	X	E	T	B
H	Q	R	U	A	A	O	N	D	N	E	N	Z	A	T	A
I	F	Y	T	V	V	B	E	W	G	N	M	F	C	A	S
L	K	E	M	F	S	W	I	B	F	W	F	D	E	W	C
L	P	T	U	A	R	W	A	T	E	P	Y	Q	B	A	A
C	J	E	W	A	T	A	L	L	I	A	L	T	T	Y	V
H	Y	C	C	B	A	T	S	T	B	B	V	R	E	D	K
E	S	K	E	E	N	A	A	E	R	A	I	E	E	Q	Y
S	T	I	K	I	N	E	Y	W	R	P	N	N	R	G	Y
Z	M	O	J	B	V	O	Q	H	A	J	O	Y	M	N	D
R	M	A	C	K	E	N	Z	I	E	U	Y	L	C	P	I

ABITIBI
ATHABASCA
CHURCHILL
FRENCH
MACKENZIE
NELSON
OTTAWA
PETAWAWA
SEVERN
ST. LAWRENCE
YUKON

ALBANY
BEAVER
FRASER
LIARD
MATTAWA
NOTTAWAY
PEACE
RED
SKEENA
STIKINE

MAZE

Canadian Crosswords

Solve the following puzzle based on the clues given!

Across

[2] A river in Canada and the United States, flowing from the YUKON TERRITORY to the Bering Sea in Alaska.

[4] A river in the Yukon Territory and the Northwest Territories, Canada, flowing from the Mackenzie Mountains to the Mackenzie River.

[7] A river in eastern Ontario and western Quebec, Canada, flowing from the Laurentian Mountains to the St. Lawrence River.

[8] A river in British Columbia, Canada, flowing from the Rocky Mountains to the Strait of Georgia.

[9] A river in the Yukon Territory and British Columbia, Canada, flowing from the Stikine Ranges to the Pacific Ocean

[10] The longest river in Canada, flowing from the Great Slave Lake in the Northwest Territories to the Arctic Ocean.

[11] A river in Alberta and British Columbia, Canada, flowing from the Rocky Mountains to the Athabasca River.

Down

[1] A river in northwestern British Columbia, Canada, flowing from the Coast Mountains to the Pacific Ocean.

[3] A river in eastern North America, flowing from the Great Lakes to the Gulf of St. Lawrence.

[5] A river in Alberta and British Columbia, Canada, flowing from the Rocky Mountains to the Peace River.

[6] A river in Manitoba, Canada, flowing from Lake Winnipeg to Hudson Bay.

Solution

Solve the following puzzle based on the clues given!

				¹S									
		²Y	U	K	O	N							
				E					³L				
				E			⁴L	I	A	R	D		
		⁵A		N					W			⁶N	
	⁷O	T	T	A	W	A		⁸F	R	A	S	E	R
		H							E			L	
		A		⁹S	T	I	K	I	N	E		S	
		B							C			O	
	¹⁰M	A	C	K	E	N	Z	I	E			N	
		S											
		C											
¹¹P	E	A	C	E									

Across

[2] A river in Canada and the United States, flowing from the YUKON TERRITORY to the Bering Sea in Alaska.

[4] A river in the Yukon Territory and the Northwest Territories, Canada, flowing from the Mackenzie Mountains to the Mackenzie River.

[7] A river in eastern Ontario and western Quebec, Canada, flowing from the Laurentian Mountains to the St. Lawrence River.

[8] A river in British Columbia, Canada, flowing from the Rocky Mountains to the Strait of Georgia.

[9] A river in the Yukon Territory and British Columbia, Canada, flowing from the Stikine Ranges to the Pacific Ocean

[10] The longest river in Canada, flowing from the Great Slave Lake in the Northwest Territories to the Arctic Ocean.

[11] A river in Alberta and British Columbia, Canada, flowing from the Rocky Mountains to the Athabasca River.

Down

[1] A river in northwestern British Columbia, Canada, flowing from the Coast Mountains to the Pacific Ocean.

[3] A river in eastern North America, flowing from the Great Lakes to the Gulf of St. Lawrence.

[5] A river in Alberta and British Columbia, Canada, flowing from the Rocky Mountains to the Peace River.

[6] A river in Manitoba, Canada, flowing from Lake Winnipeg to Hudson Bay.

Canadian Mountains

W	D	J	S	P	A	N	T	I	K	U	D	N	P	B	G
W	O	P	J	C	V	V	N	H	L	R	F	S	N	X	N
G	U	Y	O	W	Y	O	K	N	N	E	J	O	U	E	W
H	G	X	R	L	S	P	I	M	R	Q	S	A	G	J	H
L	L	B	A	B	L	F	R	F	N	B	V	R	N	K	I
D	A	D	O	N	T	I	F	E	O	T	O	Q	T	I	S
C	S	R	C	A	E	O	N	R	S	E	W	F	E	T	T
O	Q	W	O	Y	J	P	O	G	G	S	I	J	M	C	L
L	F	B	R	L	N	D	S	P	E	K	L	K	P	H	E
U	M	F	Y	O	L	O	G	A	N	R	S	S	L	E	R
M	F	C	H	E	P	H	R	E	N	B	O	Y	E	N	A
B	Q	A	Y	K	L	A	B	Z	J	V	N	O	Z	E	C
I	Q	I	S	E	S	I	B	O	G	A	R	T	F	R	F
A	A	L	B	E	R	T	A	Z	K	R	D	T	U	F	H
B	Q	A	T	H	A	B	A	S	C	A	O	V	L	E	D
S	A	N	D	F	O	R	D	A	B	J	C	O	M	U	W

ALBERTA
BOGART
COLUMBIA
CYPRESS
ELIAS
JOFFRE
LOGAN
ROBSON
SPANTIK
VAUX
WILSON

ATHABASCA
CHEPHREN
CORY
DOUGLAS
GEORGE
KITCHENER
POLLINGER
SANDFORD
TEMPLE
WHISTLER

MAZE

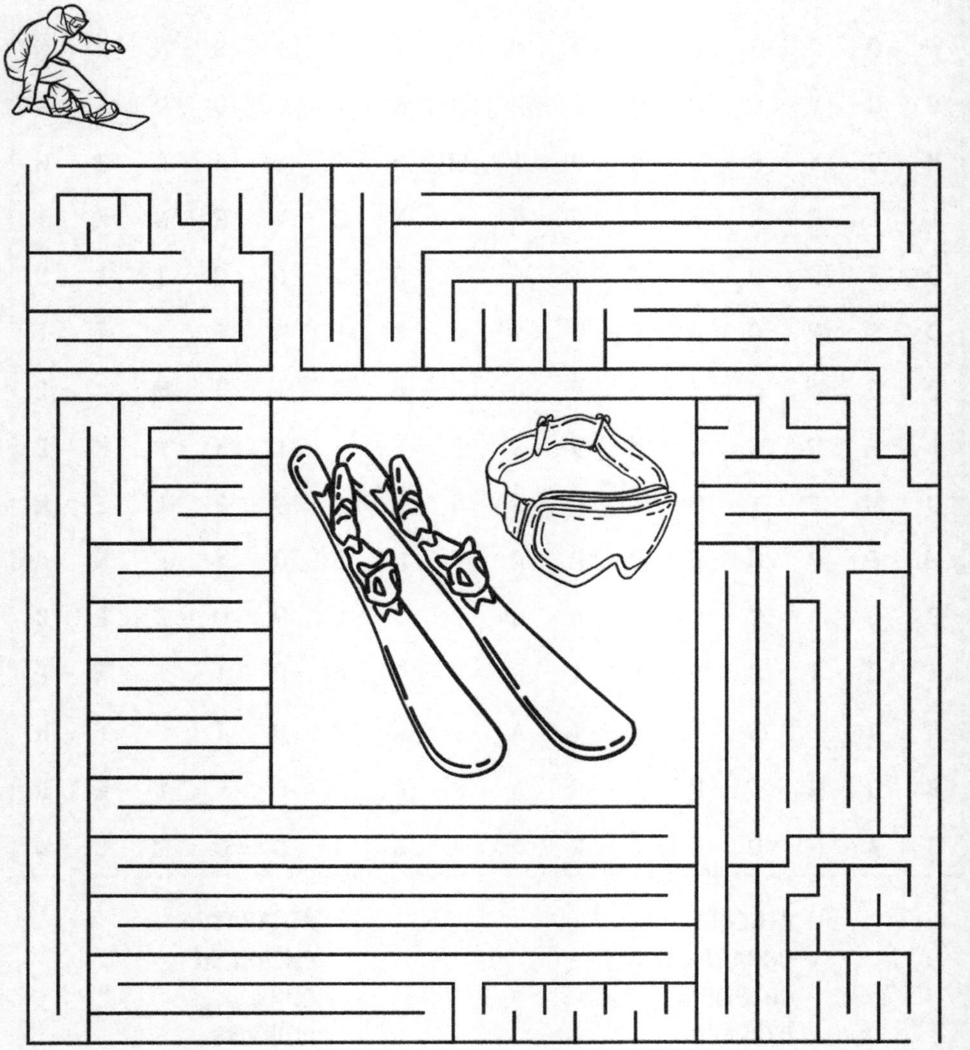

Canadian Crosswords

Solve the following puzzle based on the clues given!

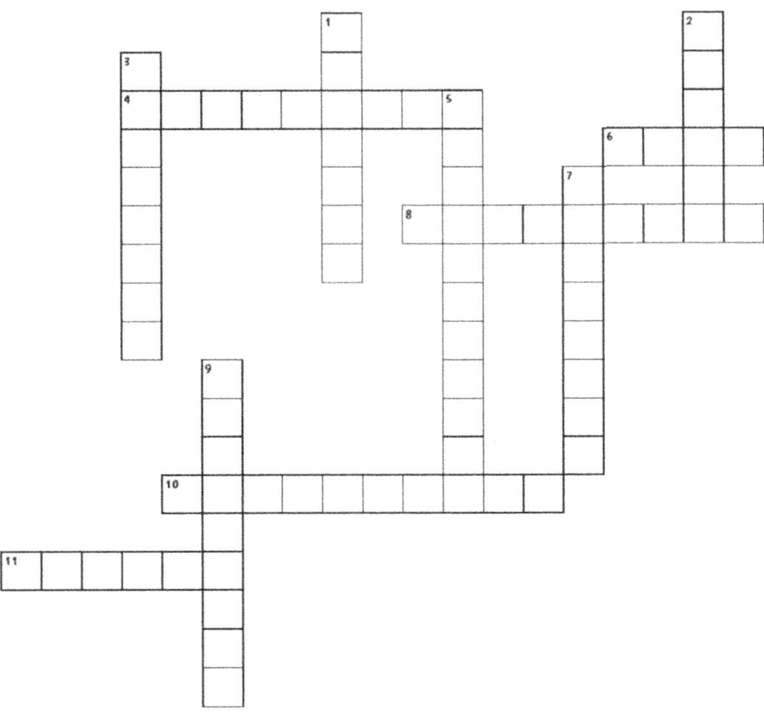

Across

[4] A mountain in Alberta, Canada, located in the Canadian Rockies.

[6] A mountain in Alberta, Canada, located in the Canadian Rockies.

[8] A mountain in Alberta, Canada, located in the Canadian Rockies.

[10] A mountain in Alberta, Canada, located in the Canadian Rockies.

[11] A mountain in Alberta, Canada, located in the Canadian Rockies.

Down

[1] A mountain in Pakistan, located in the Karakoram range.

[2] A mountain in Alberta, Canada, located in the Canadian Rockies.

[3] A mountain in Alberta, Canada, located in the Canadian Rockies.

[5] A mountain in Alberta and British Columbia, Canada, located in the Canadian Rockies.

[7] A mountain in Alberta, Canada, located in the Canadian Rockies.

[9] A mountain in Alberta, Canada, located in the Canadian Rockies.

Solution

Solve the following puzzle based on the clues given!

								1 S									2 G	
			3 S					P									E	
			4 A	T	H	A	B	A	S	C	5 A						O	
			N					N			S				6 C	O	R	Y
			D					T			S			7 C			G	
			F					I		8 K	I	T	C	H	E	N	E	R
			O					K			N			E				
			R								I			P				
			D								B			H				
					9 P						O			R				
					O						I			E				
					L						N			N				
				10 C	L	E	M	E	N	C	E	A	U					
					I													
11 W	I	L	S	O	N													
					G													
					E													
					R													

Across

[4] A mountain in Alberta, Canada, located in the Canadian Rockies.

[6] A mountain in Alberta, Canada, located in the Canadian Rockies.

[8] A mountain in Alberta, Canada, located in the Canadian Rockies.

[10] A mountain in Alberta, Canada, located in the Canadian Rockies.

[11] A mountain in Alberta, Canada, located in the Canadian Rockies.

Down

[1] A mountain in Pakistan, located in the Karakoram range.

[2] A mountain in Alberta, Canada, located in the Canadian Rockies.

[3] A mountain in Alberta, Canada, located in the Canadian Rockies.

[5] A mountain in Alberta and British Columbia, Canada, located in the Canadian Rockies.

[7] A mountain in Alberta, Canada, located in the Canadian Rockies.

[9] A mountain in Alberta, Canada, located in the Canadian Rockies.

Canadian Sports

N	D	M	A	K	F	O	O	T	B	A	L	L	N	V	U
Z	X	A	B	I	A	T	H	L	O	N	T	E	V	X	K
F	U	X	N	I	Y	C	U	R	L	I	N	G	V	R	A
R	C	A	I	G	P	D	Y	N	L	G	I	H	Y	S	U
E	S	O	C	C	E	R	F	L	Z	J	O	S	B	W	X
E	J	W	K	X	E	C	A	N	O	E	I	N	G	I	Q
S	S	T	B	A	X	B	H	Y	D	Z	S	O	S	M	A
T	D	K	T	H	E	E	E	P	O	J	K	W	I	M	S
Y	B	O	A	S	R	K	G	O	L	F	I	B	H	I	A
L	B	A	A	T	C	O	R	L	T	C	I	O	M	N	I
E	X	B	R	O	I	O	W	U	E	D	N	A	D	G	L
X	M	A	H	F	U	N	S	I	N	H	G	R	I	L	I
K	A	Y	A	K	I	N	G	R	N	N	O	D	V	U	N
R	C	R	I	C	K	E	T	T	I	G	I	I	I	T	G
O	G	L	R	U	G	B	Y	I	S	D	Q	N	N	G	A
S	M	L	A	C	R	O	S	S	E	J	O	G	G	X	Y

BASEBALL
CANOEING
CURLING
FOOTBALL
GOLF
KAYAKING
ROWING
RUNNING
SKATING
SNOWBOARDING
SWIMMING

BIATHLON
CRICKET
DIVING
FREESTYLE
HOCKEY
LACROSSE
RUGBY
SAILING
SKIING
SOCCER
TENNIS

MAZE

Canadian Crosswords

Solve the following puzzle based on the clues given!

Across

[2] A type of skiing or snowboarding that involves performing tricks and stunts on a slope or in a terrain park.

[3] A winter sport that combines cross-country skiing and rifle shooting.

[5] A sport played on ice, in which players slide stones towards a target area, trying to get as close to the center as possible.

[8] A winter sport in which participants ride down a slope on a snowboard, a narrow board with bindings that hold the feet in place.

Down

[1] A sport or activity in which people ride on a skateboard, a small board with wheels, and perform tricks and stunts.

[4] A sport or activity in which people move on ice or a smooth surface using skates, which have blades attached to the bottom.

[6] A winter sport in which participants slide down a slope on skis, long narrow boards with a flat bottom and a pointed front and back.

[7] A sport played on ice, in which two teams of skaters use sticks to try to score goals by hitting a small rubber puck into the opponent's net.

Solution

Solve the following puzzle based on the clues given!

					1 S										
					K										
					A										
2 F	R	E	E	S	T	Y	L	E							
					E										
					3 B	I	A	T	H	L	O	N			4 S
					O										K
					A										A
			5 C	U	R	L	I	N	G				6 S		T
					D								K		I
					I				7 H				I		N
				8 S	N	O	W	B	O	A	R	D	I	N	G
					G				C				N		
									K				G		
									E						
									Y						

Across

[2] A type of skiing or snowboarding that involves performing tricks and stunts on a slope or in a terrain park.

[3] A winter sport that combines cross-country skiing and rifle shooting.

[5] A sport played on ice, in which players slide stones towards a target area, trying to get as close to the center as possible.

[8] A winter sport in which participants ride down a slope on a snowboard, a narrow board with bindings that hold the feet in place.

Down

[1] A sport or activity in which people ride on a skateboard, a small board with wheels, and perform tricks and stunts.

[4] A sport or activity in which people move on ice or a smooth surface using skates, which have blades attached to the bottom.

[6] A winter sport in which participants slide down a slope on skis, long narrow boards with a flat bottom and a pointed front and back.

[7] A sport played on ice, in which two teams of skaters use sticks to try to score goals by hitting a small rubber puck into the opponent's net.

Canadian Ethnicities

T	U	L	U	T	H	U	T	T	E	R	I	T	E	Z	B
W	A	P	M	R	E	K	I	H	W	E	J	V	C	P	J
F	T	F	Y	T	T	U	S	K	D	Q	P	I	G	G	X
J	R	K	W	D	N	I	F	X	K	O	R	E	A	N	U
D	U	E	W	I	L	V	I	A	S	N	E	T	F	B	C
C	L	E	N	G	A	I	L	C	C	A	T	N	R	G	O
A	S	I	N	C	P	N	I	A	A	R	X	A	I	J	P
N	A	E	Q	V	H	D	P	D	M	M	W	M	C	I	A
A	I	S	C	U	K	I	I	I	B	T	I	E	A	R	K
D	X	R	H	F	E	A	N	A	O	L	O	S	N	A	I
I	X	N	I	O	W	N	O	N	D	W	A	E	H	N	S
A	B	M	N	S	C	O	T	T	I	S	H	T	K	I	T
N	M	W	E	N	H	P	K	Z	A	Y	F	A	I	A	A
H	L	D	S	Y	R	I	A	N	N	F	S	F	K	N	N
L	Y	G	E	L	I	S	L	A	O	T	I	A	N	M	I
C	I	E	Z	Z	J	A	P	A	N	E	S	E	T	K	N

ACADIAN
AMISH
CANADIAN
ENGLISH
FRENCH
INDIAN
IRANIAN
JAPANESE
LAOTIAN
PAKISTANI
SYRIAN

AFRICAN
CAMBODIAN
CHINESE
FILIPINO
HUTTERITE
INUIT
IRISH
KOREAN
LATIN
SCOTTISH
VIETNAMESE

MAZE

Canadian Crosswords

Solve the following puzzle based on the clues given!

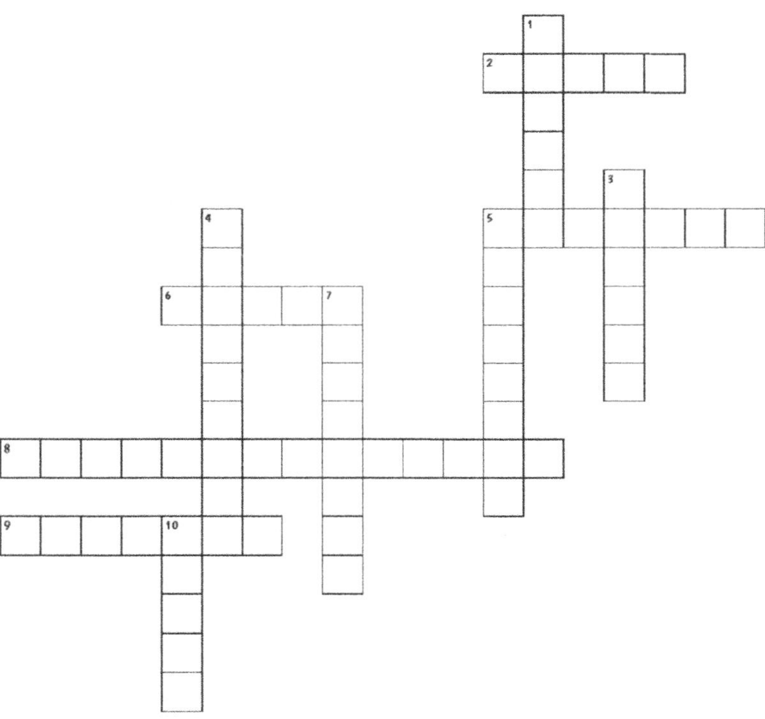

Across

[2] A person who is a native or descendant of Ireland, or who has Irish ancestry.

[5] A person who is a native or descendant of China, or who has Chinese ancestry.

[6] The Métis are a distinct Indigenous people who have a unique blend of Indigenous and European ancestry.

[8] A term used to describe people of French descent who live in

[9] A person who is a native or descendant of England, or who speaks English as their first language.

Down

[1] A person who is a native or descendant of France, or who speaks French as their first language.

[3] A person who is a native or descendant of India, or who has Indian ancestry.

[4] A term used to describe the people of Quebec, a province in eastern Canada with a predominantly French-speaking population.

[5] A person who is a citizen or resident of Canada.

[7] A person who is a native or descendant of Scotland, or who has Scottish ancestry.

[10] The Inuit are Indigenous peoples who live in the Arctic region of Canada.

Solution

Solve the following puzzle based on the clues given!

													1 F					
												2 I	R	I	S	H		
													E					
													N					
													C		3 I			
					4 Q							5 C	H	I	N	E	S	E
					U							A			D			
				6 M	É	T	I	7 S				N			I			
					B			C				A			A			
					É			O				D			N			
					C			T				I						
8 F	R	A	N	C	O	O	N	T	A	R	I	A	N					
					I			I				N						
9 E	N	G	L	10 I	S	H		S										
				N				H										
				U														
				I														
				T														

Across

[2] A person who is a native or descendant of Ireland, or who has Irish ancestry.

[5] A person who is a native or descendant of China, or who has Chinese ancestry.

[6] The Métis are a distinct Indigenous people who have a unique blend of Indigenous and European ancestry.

[8] A term used to describe people of French descent who live in

[9] A person who is a native or descendant of England, or who speaks English as their first language.

Down

[1] A person who is a native or descendant of France, or who speaks French as their first language.

[3] A person who is a native or descendant of India, or who has Indian ancestry.

[4] A term used to describe the people of Quebec, a province in eastern Canada with a predominantly French-speaking population.

[5] A person who is a citizen or resident of Canada.

[7] A person who is a native or descendant of Scotland, or who has Scottish ancestry.

[10] The Inuit are Indigenous peoples who live in the Arctic region of Canada.

MAZE

SOLUTIONS

Canadian Animals - Solution

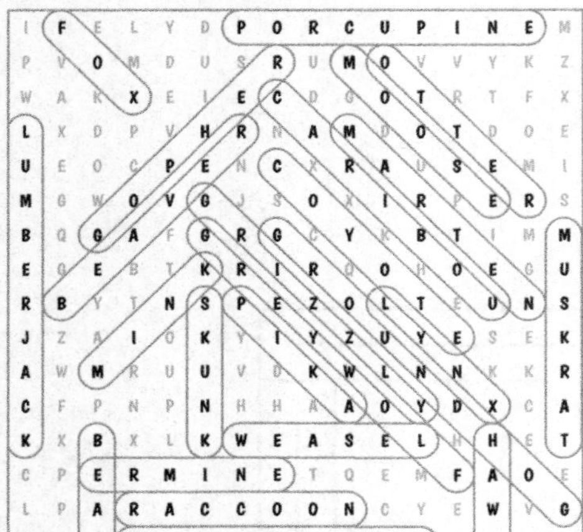

Canadian History - Solution

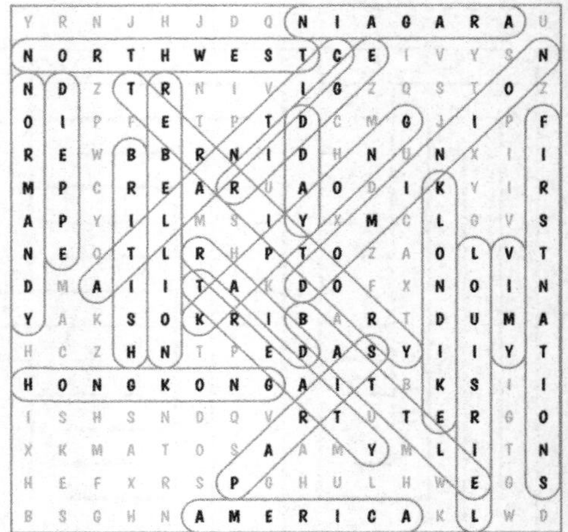

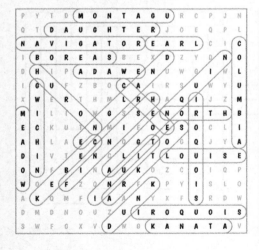

Canadian Etymology - Solution

P	Y	T	D	M	O	N	T	A	G	U	R	C	P	J	N
Q	T	D	A	U	G	H	T	E	R	J	O	E	Q	P	L
N	A	V	I	G	A	T	O	R	E	A	R	L	C	I	C
I	B	O	R	E	A	S	B	E	X	D	Z	Y	D	N	O
D	H	I	P	A	D	A	W	E	N	U	W	G	I	W	L
I	G	U	F	Z	B	O	C	A	I	R	S	U	W	Y	U
X	W	E	R	T	H	M	L	R	H	A	Q	I	J	Z	M
M	I	L	I	O	W	G	S	S	E	N	O	R	T	H	B
E	C	K	U	T	N	M	I	F	O	E	S	O	C	L	I
A	H	L	A	E	C	N	Q	G	T	O	G	Q	J	Y	A
D	I	V	T	E	N	C	L	I	T	L	O	U	I	S	E
O	N	F	B	I	N	A	U	K	O	Z	C	O	I	Q	P
W	O	E	F	Z	O	N	R	F	K	P	Y	I	S	L	O
A	K	Q	M	F	I	A	A	N	Y	X	F	S	R	D	W
D	M	D	N	O	U	Z	U	I	R	O	Q	U	O	I	S
S	W	F	G	X	V	D	W	G	K	A	N	A	T	A	V

More Canadian Etymology - Solution

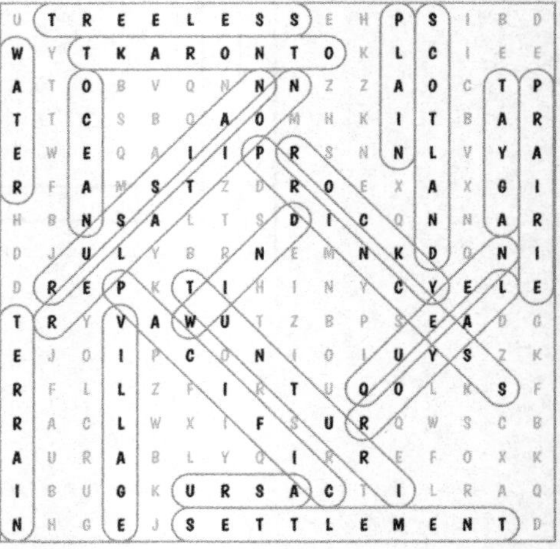

SOLUTIONS

Canadian Geography - Solution

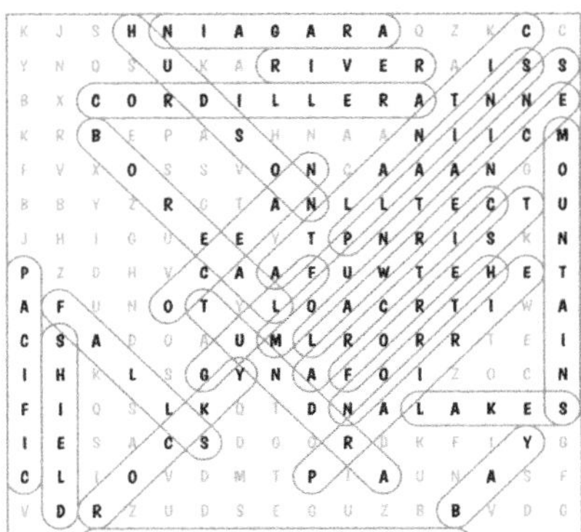

Canadian Climate - Solution

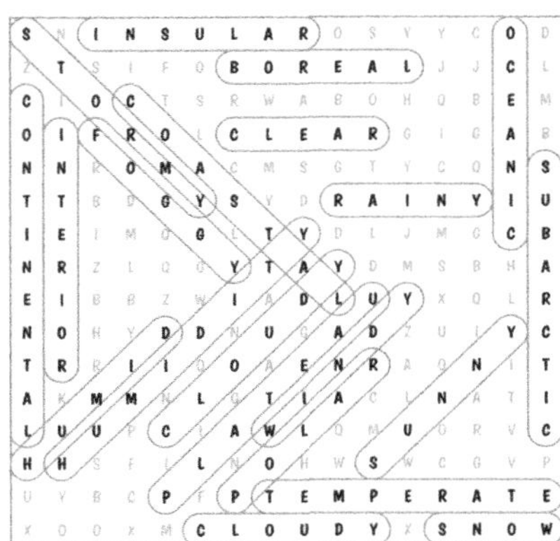

Canadian Trees - Solution

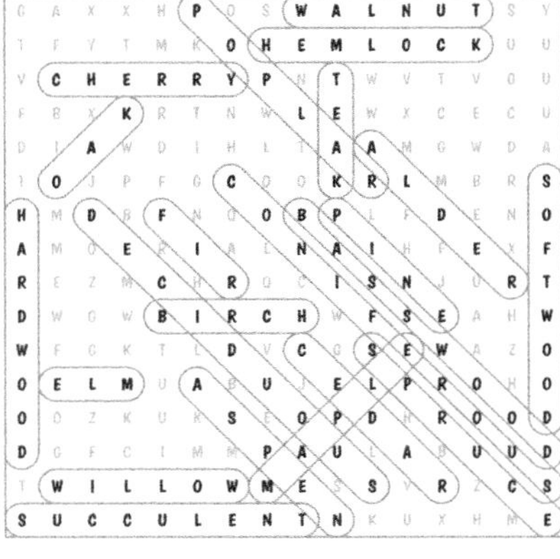

Canadian Cities - Solution

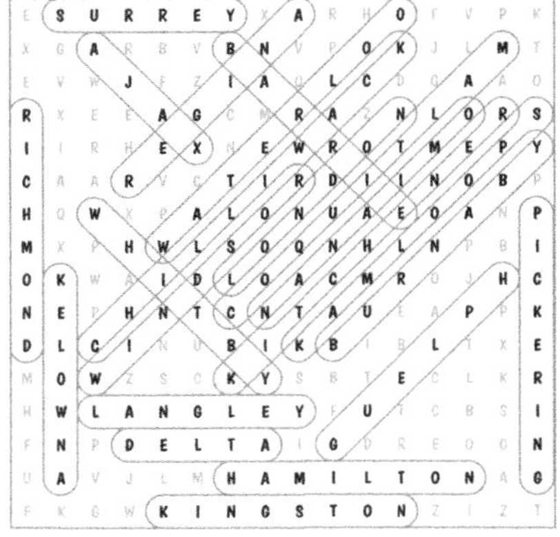

SOLUTIONS

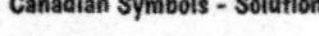

Canadian Symbols - Solution

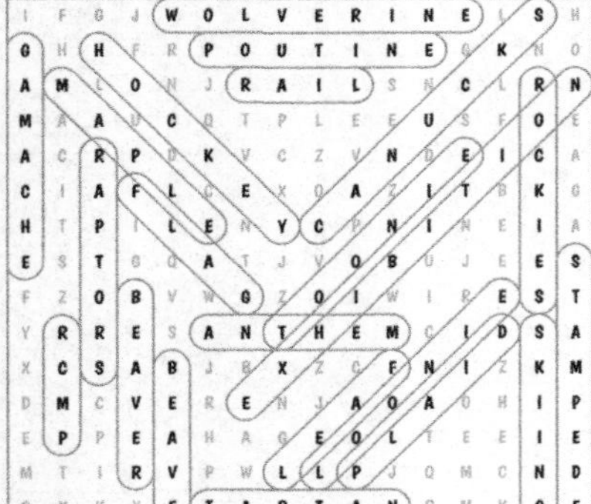

More Canadian Animals - Solution

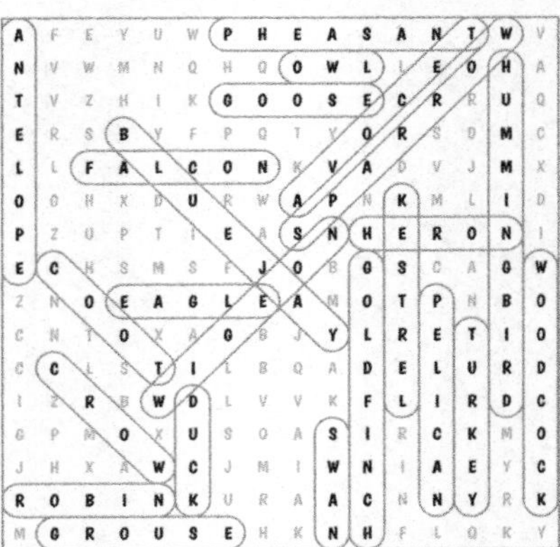

Canadian Exports - Solution

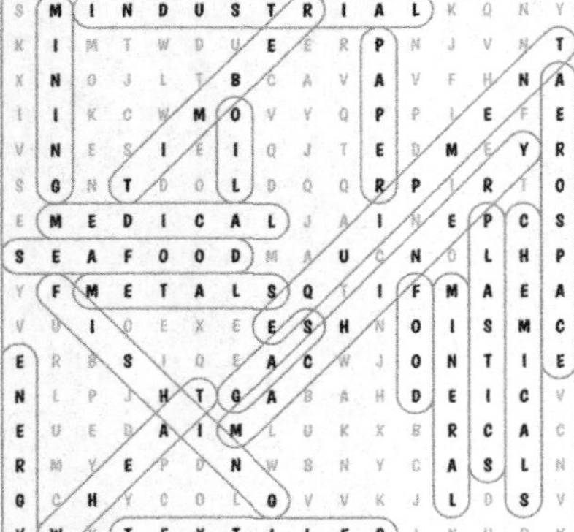

More Canadian History - Solution

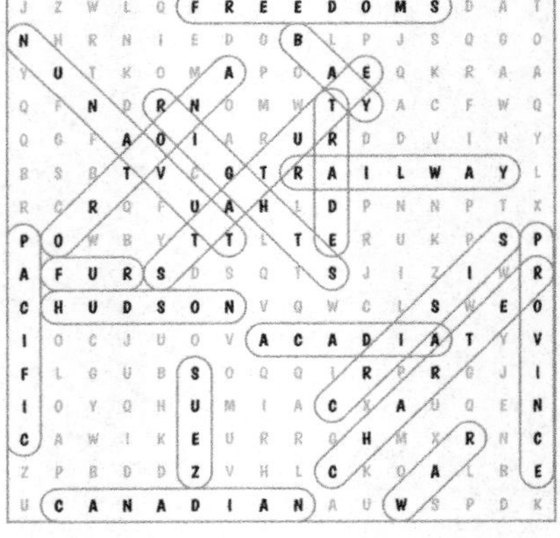

SOLUTIONS

Canadian Sports Teams - Solution

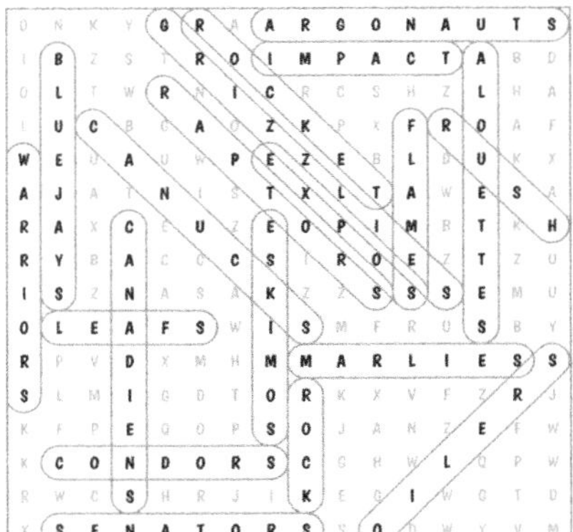

Canadian Smallest Cities - Solution

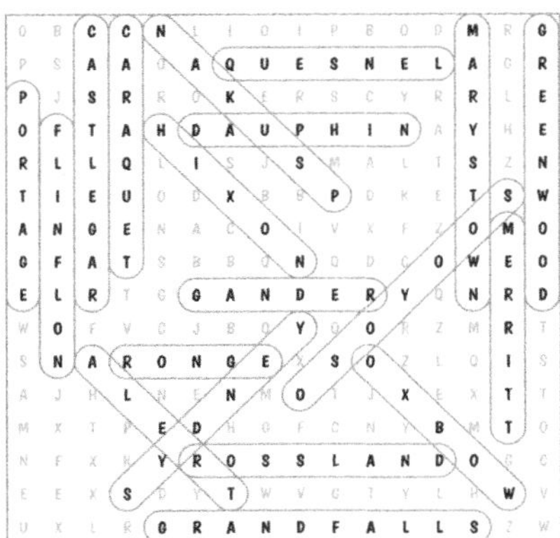

Canadian Lakes - Solution

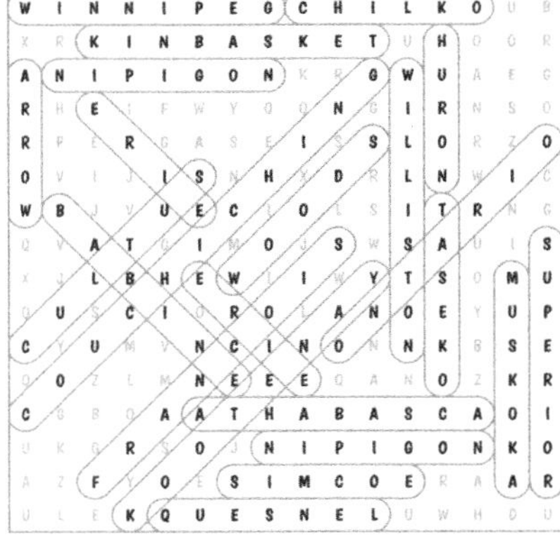

More Canadian Lakes - Solution

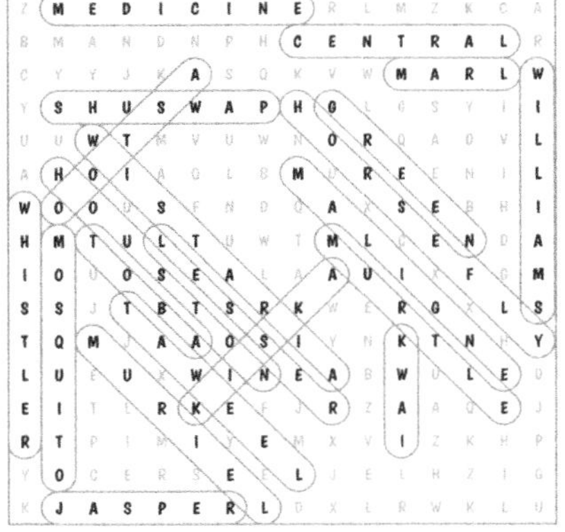

SOLUTIONS

Canadian Foods - Solution

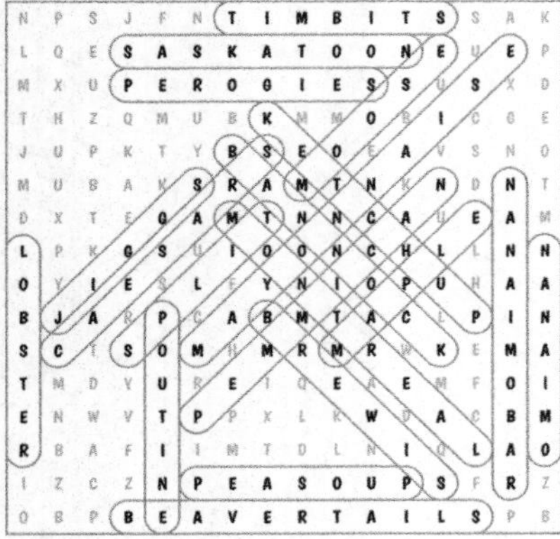

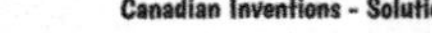

Canadian Inventions - Solution

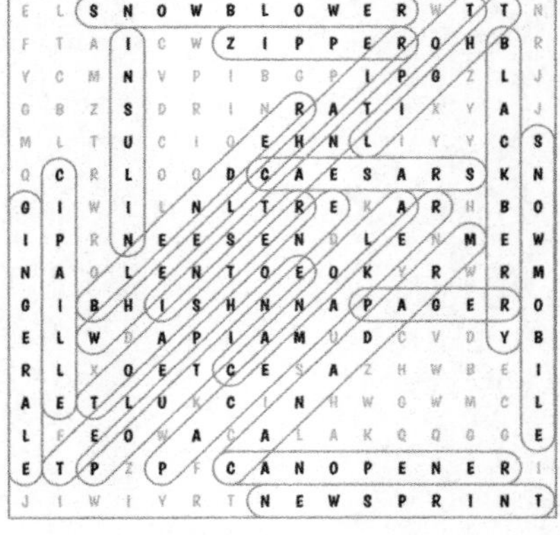

Canadian Rivers - Solution

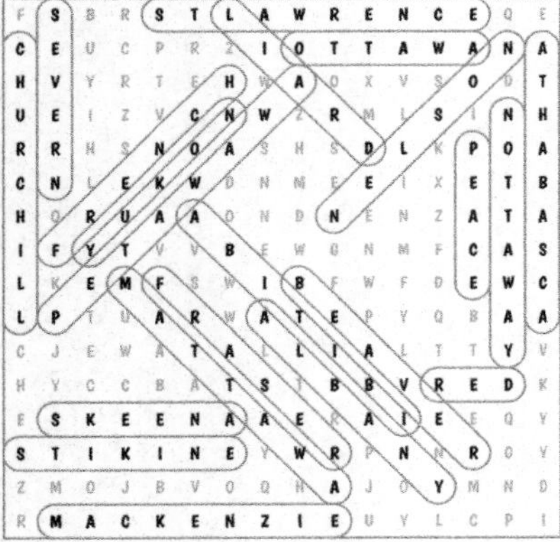

Canadian Mountains - Solution

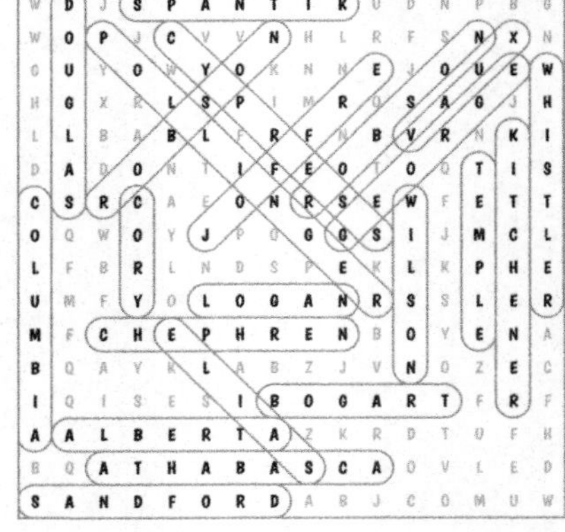

SOLUTIONS

Canadian Sports - Solution

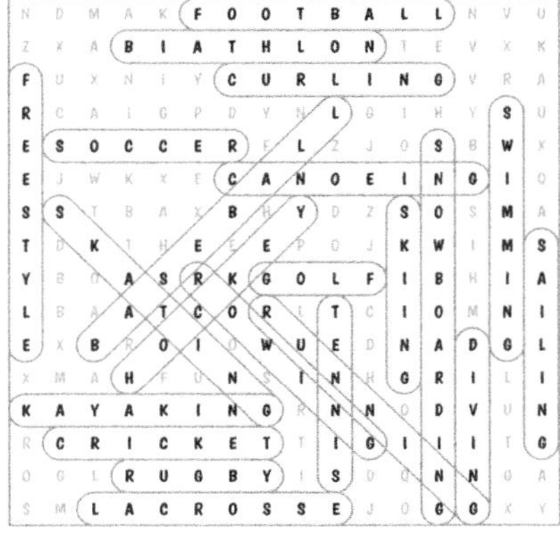

Canadian Ethnicities - Solution

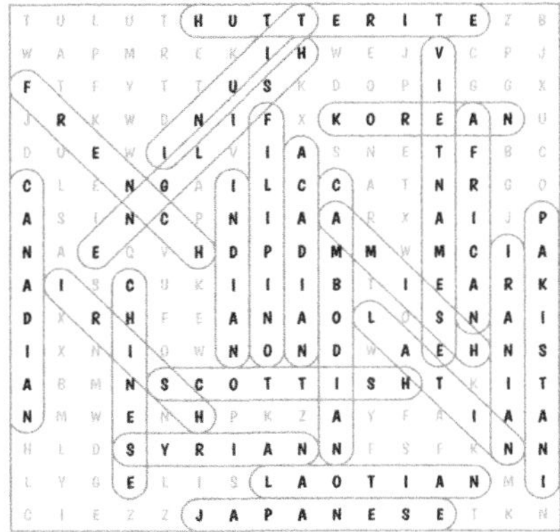

Thank You!

If you liked this Book Please Rate and Review!

Interested in more?
Explore the "Dfour Press" Author's Page
by Scanning the QR Code.

Printed in Great Britain
by Amazon

36901551R00056